Humane Medicine
A New Paradigm in Medical Education and Health Care Delivery

Humane Medicine
A New Paradigm in Medical Education and Health Care Delivery

Edited by
Richard Allen Williams, M.D.

Clinical Professor
Department of Medicine
University of California, Los Angeles, UCLA School of Medicine
Los Angeles, California
President and Chief Executive Officer, Minority Health Institute, Inc.
Beverly Hills, California

With 8 Contributing Authors

LIPPINCOTT WILLIAMS & WILKINS
A **Wolters Kluwer** Company
Philadelphia • Baltimore • New York • London
Buenos Aires • Hong Kong • Sydney • Tokyo

Acquisitions Editor: Arthur B. Giordano
Director of Manufacturing Operations: Susan Cohen
Supervising Editor: Jennifer Kullgren
Production Editor: Jane Bangley McQueen, Silverchair Science + Communications
Art Director: Kathleen Lundy
Cover Designer: Hypno Design, Inc.
Indexer: Elizabeth Willingham, Silverchair Science + Communications
Compositor: Silverchair Science + Communications
Printer: Lithoid

Printed in the United States of America

9 8 7 6 5 4 3 2 1

Library of Congress Cataloging-in-Publication Data
Humane medicine : a new paradigm in medical education and health care
    delivery / editor, Richard Allen Williams.
        p.   cm.
    Includes bibliographical references and index.
    ISBN 0-7817-2030-3
    1. Social medicine. 2. Minorities--Medical care. 3. Minorities-
-Health and hygiene. 4. Holistic medicine. I. Williams, Richard
Allen, 1936-   .
RA418.H847 1998
362.1--dc21   98-43507
                                                        CIP

Care has been taken to confirm the accuracy of the information presented and to describe generally accepted practices. However, the authors, editors, and publisher are not responsible for errors or omissions or for any consequences from application of the information in this book and make no warranty, expressed or implied, with respect to the contents of the publication.

The authors, editors, and publisher have exerted every effort to ensure that drug selection and dosages set forth in this text are in accordance with current recommendations and practice at the time of publication. However, in view of ongoing research, changes in government regulations, and the constant flow of information relating to drug therapy and drug reactions, the reader is urged to check the package insert for each drug for any change in indications and dosage and for added warnings and precautions. This is particularly important when the recommended agent is a new or infrequently employed drug.

Some drugs and medical devices presented in this publication have Food and Drug Administration (FDA) clearance for limited use in restricted research settings. It is the responsibility of health care providers to ascertain the FDA status of each drug or device planned for use in their clinical practice.

The publishers have made every effort to trace the copyright holders for borrowed material. If they have inadvertently overlooked any, they will be pleased to make the necessary arrangements at the first opportunity.

To my granddaughters, Annalisa and Kelsea

Contents

Contributing Authors ix

Preface xi

Acknowledgments xv

1. Race, Ethnicity, Culture, and Religion in Medicine 1
   Richard Allen Williams

2. Molecular Genetics for the Clinical Cardiologist 17
   Michael D. Schneider

3. A Biopsychosocial Perspective: Socioeconomic
   Influences on Health 29
   Norman B. Anderson

4. Substance Abuse: Health Care Implications 39
   Louis L. Cregler

5. Role of Medical Ethics in the Training of Physicians 47
   Marian Gray Secundy

6. Medical and Legal Issues 53
   B. Waine Kong, Stephanie Kong, and Jillian Kong-Sivert

7. Nutritional Factors in the Health of Minority Populations 63
   Shiriki K. Kumanyika

8. Management of Hypertension in Minorities 73
   Richard Allen Williams

9. Women's Health Issues 85
   Anne L. Taylor

Subject Index 93

Contributing Authors

Norman B. Anderson, Ph.D. *Director, Office of Behavioral and Social Sciences Research, Office of the Director, National Institutes of Health, One Center Drive, Bethesda, Maryland 20892; Associate Professor, Departments of Psychology and Psychiatry, Duke University, Durham, North Carolina 27710; and President (1998–1999), Society of Behavioral Medicine, Bethesda, Maryland 20814*

Louis L. Cregler, M.D., F.A.C.P., F.A.C.C. *Deputy Dean, Academic Affairs, and Professor, Department of Medicine, City University of New York Medical School, 138 Street and Convent Avenue, New York, New York 10031; and Attending Physician/Cardiology, Department of Medicine, Maimonides Medical Center, 4802 Tenth Avenue, Brooklyn, New York 11219*

B. Waine Kong, Ph.D., J.D. *Chief Executive Officer, Association of Black Cardiologists, Inc., 225 Peachtree Street, Northeast, Atlanta, Georgia 30310*

Stephanie Kong, M.D. *President, Metrohealth, 3151 Rilman Road, Northwest, Atlanta, Georgia 30327*

Jillian Kong-Sivert *Legal Assistant, Office of Senator Barbara McKulski, U.S. Senate, Washington, D.C. 20002*

Shiriki K. Kumanyika, Ph.D., R.D., M.P.H. *Professor and Head, Department of Human Nutrition and Dietetics, College of Health and Human Development Sciences, University of Illinois College of Medicine, 1919 West Taylor Street, Chicago, Illinois 60612*

Michael D. Schneider, M.D. *Professor, Departments of Medicine, Cell Biology, and Molecular Biology and Biophysics, Molecular Cardiology Unit, Baylor College of Medicine, 1 Baylor Plaza, Houston, Texas 77030*

Marian Gray Secundy, Ph.D. *Professor, Department of Community Health and Family Practice, and Director, Program in Clinical Ethics, Howard University College of Medicine, 520 West Street, Northwest, Washington, D.C. 20059*

Anne L. Taylor, M.D. *Associate Professor, Department of Internal Medicine, and Vice Chair, Women's Health Programs, Department of Medicine, Division of Cardiology, Case Western Reserve University School of Medicine, 10900 Euclid Avenue, Cleveland, Ohio 44106*

Richard Allen Williams, M.D. *Clinical Professor, Department of Medicine, University of California, Los Angeles, UCLA School of Medicine, Los Angeles, California 90024; and President and Chief Executive Officer, Minority Health Institute, Inc., 8306 Wilshire Boulevard, Beverly Hills, California 90211*

Preface

In February 1998, the First Symposium on Humane Medicine was held in Keystone, Colorado. Some of the best academic minds in medicine met with a group of physicians in private practice to develop a methodology for creating and implementing a revised system of medical practice and medical education. Papers presented by scholars from various areas of medicine were presented to the assembled clinical consultants and were discussed over 3 days. Those lectures form the basis of the chapters in *Humane Medicine: A New Paradigm in Medical Education and Health Care Delivery*, which is the first in a series on humane medicine.

This book is the second phase of an attempt to impress on the medical community that it should alter its approach to delivering health care to those American citizens who most require it: disadvantaged and minority populations, women, the elderly, the disabled, and other special subgroups who too often receive less than the highest quality of medical attention. In the first phase, which I initiated in 1975 with publication of the *Textbook of Black-Related Diseases*, a large body of information about differences in disease manifestations between blacks and whites was assembled. The thesis was that black patients as a group require a special approach to diagnosis, evaluation, and treatment of disease because of the differences documented in the text.

Since its publication, this thesis has been largely accepted, leading to a better appreciation of the fact that certain drugs do not work as well in blacks as in whites, that some diseases have a more severe effect on blacks, and that there are substantial differences in mortality rates between blacks and whites for almost every medical disorder. Most important, it is now well recognized that a significant gap exists between blacks and whites in regard to health care delivery, specifically the quality of that care. It is also accepted that health data that has been accumulated on whites is not completely transferable to blacks.

Despite the huge body of information gathered and the emphasis placed on the need to devise strategies to eliminate the health care gap that adversely affects minorities, the health status of minority populations still lags at least 30 years behind that of whites in the United States, and the gap appears to be widening. Why? I believe it is because there has been little transition from issues to action. It is not enough merely to document and call attention to problems that exist with the expectation that those problems will be acted on once recognized.

How can the transition from issues to action be accomplished? Health care providers must first be fully educated, and then they must be sensitized regarding cultural, ethnic, racial, gender, chronologic, religious, and other factors that play an integral role in how well or how poorly patients respond to medical ministrations. That is what this book is all about.

I coined the term *humane medicine* to indicate that there must be more to the practice of medicine than just treatment of illness. First and foremost, it must be acknowledged that it is the patient and his or her illness, not just the medical disorder, that should be the focus of physicians' attention. As practitioners, we should view the patient as a complex collection of many disparate factors to be sorted through, analyzed, evaluated, and ultimately treated. Thus, the patient should be regarded holistically rather than viewed simply as a macroorganism with a physical malfunction in need of repair. Giving the patient this extra measure of consideration and taking care to be sensitive to his or her special cultural, racial, religious, or other characteristics is an attitude that lies at the center of humane medicine. However, such an attitude is rarely seen and is not regularly taught in medical schools. Most schools of medicine do not include anything more than lip-service exposure to learning how to approach patients in a proper manner. Because of this deficit, practitioners emerge from these institutions with treatment skills that are less than patient-friendly. This is an obvious paradox in a field that should place patients at the top of the list of priorities.

Humane medicine also implies compassion for the patient and genuine concern about the problems presented. True comprehension of the patient's health status does not come to the physician unless these ingredients are part of his or her repertoire. Although it is not necessary for physicians to identify completely with patients' problems or to be overly altruistic, a healthy dose of empathy goes a long way to convince patients that physicians are their partners in controlling or curing their specific illness.

We do a very good job teaching medicine in the United States, however, and we have arguably the best health care system in the world. Why, then, do we need something like humane medicine? If medicine is not broken, why fix it? In truth, there is a paradox here. The United States does have a superb medical system, technologically speaking. We are experts at diagnosing new diseases, eliminating old ones, inventing new treatments, developing novel drugs, and improving the use of drugs and treatments already available. The problem is not with technology; rather, the problem is with application of medical tools to help the very patients for whom they were developed. Being in possession of knowledge and applying that knowledge are not the same thing. Special mechanisms must be created that will allow brilliantly spawned technology to be used properly. Perhaps this paradox is best expressed by poetic means:

> Upon this gifted age, in its dark hour,
> Rains from the sky a meteoric shower
> Of facts . . . they lie unquestioned, uncombined,
> Wisdom enough to leech us of our ill
> Is daily spun, but there exists no loom
> To weave it into fabric, . . .
>   —Edna St. Vincent Millay, "Huntsman, What Quarry?"

The chief purpose of this book is to create the loom that will weave the myriad facts and statistics into the fabric of high-quality health care. What is needed is development of a medical school curriculum of humane medicine containing infrequently taught subjects, such as gerontology; women's health issues; molecular biology; socioeconomics; psychiatric perspectives; substance abuse; nutrition; race, ethnicity, culture, and religion in medicine; hypertension in minorities; biomedical ethics; medical and legal issues; violence; and many other neglected topics, to build a patient-friendly system that will improve the health of the most needy in U.S. society. It is hoped that distribution of this book to medical schools will be followed by a transition from the symposium's think-tank format to incorporation of the ideas into schools' curriculum revision plans. It is also hoped that the book will encourage changes in the way physicians practice medicine in a diverse, multicultural society.

Richard Allen Williams

Acknowledgments

Special thanks are due to a number of people who have helped me bring the concept of humane medicine into being. The most important person is Dr. Howard Besbris, medical information scientist for Astra Pharmaceuticals, who has been the sounding board, counselor, and gentle critic that I needed to help bring this idea to market. Warren Cooper, M.D., an executive at Astra, was also very instrumental in obtaining the funding for the symposium on which this book is based. I will never forget our stroll in London's Hyde Park as we discussed the prospects, problems, and promise associated with the development of such a radical concept. As Victor Hugo said, more powerful than all the armies of the world is an idea whose time has come. It is to the credit of Dr. Cooper and Astra Pharmaceuticals that they recognized that this was the time for the birth of humane medicine. Although no financial gain will likely come to them for promulgating this idea, they are committed to it.

Others who deserve to be recognized for their interest and help are Dr. Sylvia LaFair; Larrye Loss; Nancy Tenenbaum; Jamie Reisch; Ernestine Blue; all of the people at Lippincott Williams & Wilkins, my patient publisher, including Art Giordano and Jennifer Kullgren; and Jane Bangley McQueen of Silverchair Science + Communications. Because future iterations of this book are anticipated based on other symposia, it is comforting to know that I will have an opportunity to work with them again. I hope this feeling is mutual.

1

Race, Ethnicity, Culture, and Religion in Medicine

Richard Allen Williams

Department of Medicine, University of California, Los Angeles, UCLA School of Medicine, Los Angeles, California 90024, and Minority Health Institute, Inc., Beverly Hills, California 90211

It is difficult and complicated to describe how race, ethnicity, culture, and religion, four societal categories that help to delineate similarities and differences between humans, affect medical science and clinical practice. These concepts are hard to express in concrete terms, and there is no general agreement on their definitions, meanings, importance, and applicability. I have attempted to provide some insights into the impact of each of these categories on medicine, however, and I cite and provide a sampling of the available evidence and sources of my contentions, which come from various historical, literary, statistical, epidemiologic, and experimental sources. Consideration of these matters is significant in a discussion of humaneness in medicine, because if our practice of medicine is negatively influenced by these factors, due either to our ignorance of their importance or to malicious intent, then it must be altered so that our patients may benefit.

DEFINITION OF TERMS

The Concept of Race

The word *race*, derived from the Latin *generatio* (a begetting), is a complex of semantic ambiguities, according to anthropologist Elizabeth S. Watts (1). It is a taxonomic expression that is useful for classification because it subdivides the human species (*Homo sapiens*) into groups based on phenotypic similarities such as color and texture of hair, color of skin and eyes, facial features, and body proportions. It also distinguishes populations by the relative frequency of certain genes (2). Three primary divisions are described by most authorities: Caucasian (white), Negroid (black), and Mongoloid (yellow, Asian), but other classifications have been offered by other authorities (Table 1-1). The attempt to organize humankind into different groups based on phenotypic characteristics originated with the

TABLE 1-1. *Some racial classifications of man from the eighteenth century to the present*

Blumenbach (1781)	Huxley (1870)	Boyd (1950)	Garn (1961)	Coon (1962)	Brues (1977)
Caucasian	Xanthocroid	Caucasoid (early European)	European	Caucasoid	Caucasoid
—	Melanocroid	—	Indian	—	—
Ethiopian	Negroid	Negroid	African	Congoid	Negroid
—	—	—	—	Capoid	—
Mongolian	Mongoloid	Mongoloid	Asiatic	Mongoloid	Mongoloid
American	—	American Indian	Amerindian	—	—
—	—	—	Polynesian	—	—
—	—	—	Micronesian	—	—
Malay	—	—	Melanesian	—	—
—	Australoid	Australoid	Australian	Australoid	Australoid

From ref. 1, with permission.

Swedish taxonomist Linnaeus (Karl von Linne) in his monumental work, *Systema Naturae* (*A General System of Nature*), written in 1735 (Fig. 1-1). In the typologic classification constructed by Linnaeus, Caucasians are held in the highest regard and Negroid types in the lowest. The descriptions of Negroid types are unflattering, and it is obvious that the race of the classifier has determined who is considered admirable and who is not.

Several other attempts have been made to classify man on a biological basis, and skin color has been the principal physical characteristic used for classification. Ancient Greek mythology related that differences in skin color throughout the world were created when the sun god, Helios, allowed his son Phaeton to drive the sun chariot. Phaeton, an erratic driver, flew too close to certain parts of the earth, causing the residents to become burnished, and too far away from other areas, causing people there to have blanched skin and the environment to be cold. But it was humans, not the gods, who decided how to rank people according to the color of their skin. Anthropologists such as Carlton Coon have published insulting treatises that demean certain groups (e.g., blacks) while exalting others (e.g., whites) using skin color as the principal criterion. Even before Coon's pronouncements, there were efforts to place blacks in a different species category than whites.

The pseudoscience of phrenology fomented considerable scientific dissension; through it, medicine aided and abetted the proslavery forces in defending their bigoted attitudes. The pinnacle of their endeavors came on the cold night of February 8, 1848, when the distinguished fellows of the Academy of Natural Science of Philadelphia met to hear a lecture delivered by their most revered member, the eminent craniologist Dr. Samuel George Morton. Dr. Morton, commenting on the physical features of an 18-year-old Hottentot boy who had been sent to him from South Africa as a subject for scientific investigation, described the young man's head as

MAMMALIA.

ORDER I. PRIMATES.

Fore-teeth cutting; upper 4, parallel; teats 2 pectoral.

1. HOMO.

Sapiens. Diurnal; varying by education and situation.

2. Four-footed, mute, hairy.   *Wild Man.*
3. Copper-coloured, choleric, erect.   *American.*
   Hair black, straight, thick; *nostrils* wide, *face* harsh; *beard* scanty; *obstinate*, content free. *Paints* himself with fine red lines. *Regulated* by customs.
4. Fair, sanguine, brawny.   *European.*
   Hair yellow, brown, flowing; *eyes* blue; *gentle*, acute, inventive. *Covered* with close vestments. *Governed* by laws.
5. Sooty, melancholy, rigid.   *Asiatic.*
   Hair black; *eyes* dark; *severe*, haughty, covetous. *Covered* with loose garments. *Governed* by opinions.
6. Black, phlegmatic, relaxed.   *African.*
   Hair black, frizzled; *skin* silky; *nose* flat; *lips* tumid; *crafty*, indolent, negligent. *Anoints* himself with grease. *Governed* by caprice.

Monstrosus Varying by climate or art.

1. Small, active, timid.   *Mountaineer.*
2. Large, indolent.   *Patagonian.*
3. Less fertile.   *Hottentot.*
4. Beardless.   *American.*
5. Head conic.   *Chinese.*
6. Head flattened.   *Canadian.*

The anatomical, physiological, natural, moral, civil and social histories of man, are best described by their respective writers.

Vol. I —C   2. SIMIA.

FIG. 1-1. Racial classification of man published by Linnaeus. (From ref. 1, with permission.)

completely foreign to the European concept of the ideal physical features for the human species (3). Morton had already written his epic *Crania Americana* in 1839, in which he purported to demonstrate that measurements of the human skull revealed marked differences between racial types, with whites having the largest skulls, Indians the next largest, and blacks the smallest (Table 1-2). He invited the inference that the intelligence of a race was directly proportional to brain size, which was directly proportional to skull capacity. His theories were taught in medical schools and accepted and discussed by the most outstanding physicians and scientists of the day, including Dr. Charles Meigs, Dr. John Collins Warren, and Dr. Louis Agassiz of Harvard. Advocates of slavery used Morton's work in their attempts to keep blacks,

TABLE 1-2. *Skull sizes by race*

Races	Number of skulls	Mean internal capacity (cu in.)	Largest in series (cu in.)
Caucasian	52	87	109
Mongolian	10	83	93
Malay	18	81	89
American	147	80	100
Ethiopian	29	78	94

From ref. 3, with permission.

whom they considered mentally inferior, enslaved. It also comforted any fears that slave owners might have about the immorality of one of God's children holding his brothers, men and women of the same species, in bondage.

Another example of how science aided slavery was the infamous U.S. Census of 1840. Dr. Edward Jarvis, a Boston physician, made the startling discovery that the sixth census reported the incidence of insanity among free blacks in the North to be 1.0 in 162.4, which was extraordinarily high, whereas it was only 1 in 1,558 among slaves in the South (4). There seemed to be a correlation between lunacy and latitude among blacks, with an increased frequency of insanity in the territory from Mississippi to Maine, where every fourteenth black was noted to be either a lunatic or an idiot. The proslavery forces claimed that here was evidence that bondage was protective of blacks' sanity and that blacks could not compete in a free society without going completely mad. Determining by detailed analysis that the figures on allegedly insane blacks in many towns exceeded the total number of blacks living there, Dr. Jarvis exposed the statistics as fraudulent. Historians suspect that the fraud was perpetrated by J. C. Calhoun of South Carolina, who, as secretary of the treasury, was in charge of the census. The bogus scientific statistics were used in scholarly publications to document so-called black mental inferiority.

These are but two examples of how the concept of race has been distorted and misused to advance bias in medicine against certain groups and how racism can evolve when superficial distinctions between peoples are exploited with ill intent. There should be no doubt that there is a link between race, racism, and health. Whenever the poor health status of blacks is cited as a problem requiring society's attention and intervention, apologists for the majority population give excuses that place blame on the victims. For example, Cartwright wrote in the *New Orleans Medical and Surgical Journal* in 1851 that the difference in health status between whites and blacks was due to the perception that "the Negro's brain and nerves, the chyle and all the humora are tinctured with a shade of pervading darkness" (3). And Weiss, writing in the *American Heart Journal* in 1939 on the perceived infrequency of angina pectoris in the black race, held that blacks experienced less chest discomfort because "more than moronic intelligence" is necessary to perceive the sensation of pain (5).

It is apparent that racism still flourishes in medicine. As recently as 1993, articles were published in the *New England Journal of Medicine* and elsewhere on such subjects as racial differences in the incidence of cardiac arrest and subsequent survival (6), racial differences in the use of invasive cardiovascular procedures (7), the outcome of coronary artery bypass grafting in blacks (8), and the poorer prognosis of black patients after discharge from the hospital following myocardial infarction (9). Regarding the use of invasive procedures, such as cardiac catheterization, coronary angioplasty, and coronary artery bypass surgery, when financial factors were removed as confounding elements in a study of 428,300 black and white patients in the Veterans Administration hospital system in which care is free and doctors are salaried, a significant difference still occurred, with these procedures being used much less frequently in blacks (7). According to the author, "Our data, coupled with the results of previous studies, suggest the existence of race-related inequities in our health care system" (7). In an editorial on the less frequent use of invasive cardiovascular procedures in blacks and the lower survival rate from cardiac arrest for blacks, Ayanian (10) stated, "These disparities are rooted in the unequal social and economic opportunities available to blacks in a predominantly white society." These are documented, clear, and unequivocal evidence of racism in medicine, rather than of some innate factors incidental to the patients' race.

Race should be understood to be merely a term of convenience for categorizing people according to shared physical and, to some extent, genetic characteristics. Such taxonomic labels can be useful, but they can also lead to dangerous stereotyping and bias.

The Concept of Ethnicity

To escape the difficulties associated with the term *race*, Ashley Montagu invented a new term in 1964, *ethnic group* (11). Because *ethnic* implies membership in a socially rather than biologically defined group, the hope is that the bias and bigotry generated by *race* can be avoided by using *ethnic group* and *ethnicity*. It makes more sense, therefore, for us to use the ethnically relevant term *African-American* than the biologically related expression *black*.

However, simply changing the focus from the biological to the sociologic characteristics of a population group does not eliminate bias. It might be argued that most cases of racial discrimination are actually instances of social discrimination, although this renders the bias no less onerous. The common denominator in racial and ethnic bias is the bigoted perception, developed by one group about another group that differs in some way, that the first, bigoted group is superior and exalted. Science and medicine are often used to document these differences, as in the phrenology example described earlier. They can serve as catalysts, helping to convince people who are in the more powerful, controlling group to accept the subjugation of others to the demands, denial of access to care, brutality, enslavement, and other indignities to which racial and ethnic minorities, for instance, are exposed.

The bigot is somehow absolved of guilt if the people who are tortured, murdered, exploited, enslaved, or provided substandard treatments are seen as different and inferior. It is in the nature of prejudice, as described by Harvard sociologist Gordon Allport, to blame the subjugated, powerless group for the trials and tribulations with which it is beset (12). This prejudicial process was seen in the writings of Wilhelm Schallmeyer in Germany (1857–1919), who united social darwinism with the theory of innate degeneracy, which held that mental retardation, shortsightedness, mental illness, and other negative characteristics were caused by a degenerate constitution. In doing so, he provided a rationale for managing human reproduction that was later used by the Nazis against the Jews. Similar pronouncements were made by Fritz Lenz, a scientific theorist for Nazi racial thought, as documented by Proctor (13). Other examples are given by Lifton (14) and Müller-Hill (15). In more recent years, the eugenics and racial hygiene theories of Harvard professor Benjamin Davis, the writings of Harvard professor Richard Herrnstein and others regarding alleged black intellectual inferiority, and the bell curve thesis (also authored at Harvard) have joined the works of Jensen, Eysenck, and others in assaulting the integrity of black mental health and intellectual capacity.

It is obvious, therefore, that simply substituting terms (e.g., *ethnic group* or *ethnicity* for *race*) does not eliminate racism. As medical professionals, we must develop a sensitivity regarding these issues that will help us to manage our patients according to the special needs and considerations that they require as members of discrete racial or ethnic groups. Sometimes, we can become educated on these matters by listening to patients or by reading nonphysician observers and writers such as Kirk Johnson (16).

The Concept of Culture

According to Fabrega, the term *culture* involves a group's system of social symbols and the meanings of those symbols (17). Culture, then, looks beyond what Fabrega calls the *biomedical portrait of disease* and involves the traditions, mores, customs, rituals, and patterns that are peculiar to a distinct group of people. This may have tremendous effects on the view of health care held by people in a given culture, and it can affect their understanding, acceptance, and use of the health care system presented to them. Cultural factors may also determine the extent to which an ill person understands his or her disease; as physicians, we tend to explain illness on an organic basis (i.e., in terms of some infectious or other process affecting the brain, heart, liver, and so forth), but a patient who is from the Maya Indian town of Zinacantan in the highlands of Chiapas, Mexico, may not be able to understand illness in the Western orthodox medical context, instead understanding disease as a foreign process or spirit entering the body (16). A patient who believes in voodoo medicine and who has been treated with kerosene-soaked sugar cubes for a cold by a voodoo practitioner may not understand that he or she has developed serious renal disease because of this treatment and needs urgent medical attention to reverse it.

There are many considerations surrounding the complex nature of culture and its impact on health care. Clinicians should be thoroughly educated about the cultural norms that their patients observe and should work with the patient's system of cultural values, rather than against it or entirely outside of it.

The Concept of Religion

Religion is the most delicate of the four concepts analyzed here. The subtlety of its nature derives from the very meaning of *religion*, which may be defined as a system of beliefs based on a group's faith in the power of a supreme being or beings. The positive

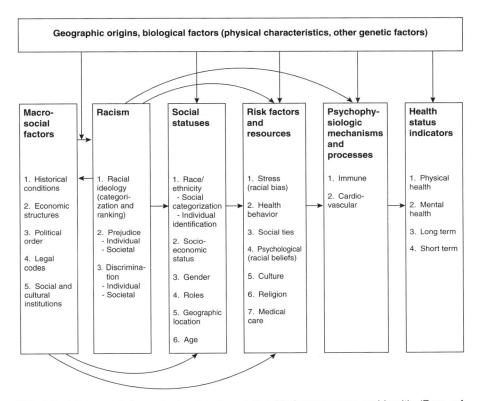

FIG. 1-2. A framework for understanding the relationship between race and health. (From ref. 17, with permission.)

impact of religion on medicine and science has been tremendous; however, it might also be said that religion has obstructed their advance. For instance, vivisection or dissection of the human body was forbidden for centuries in Europe, and it was not until Andreas Vesalius published *De Humanis Corporis Fabrica* (*Structure of the Human Body*) in 1543 that human anatomy was studied in a thorough manner (18). Religion still has a pervasive influence on the practice of medicine today. The most noteworthy example is the rejection of blood transfusions by Jehovah's Witnesses, which has led to the development of techniques for bloodless surgery and to the wider use of blood substitutes to accommodate patients who are subject to religious restrictions.

A Unifying View of Race, Ethnicity, Culture, and Religion in Medicine

There is considerable overlap between the four categories just discussed. Figure 1-2 summarizes this interdigitation; it shows the interrelation between race and health, but it also demonstrates that all of the factors cited are codependent variables that every physician should take into account in attempting to provide optimal, sensitive care (19).

FIFTY CENTURIES OF BLACKS IN MEDICINE

This section provides a brief survey of the importance of black physicians to the field of medicine. It begins with Imhotep, an Egyptian from sub-Saharan Africa who lived in Egypt in approximately 3000 B.C., during the Third Dynasty. Imhotep was renowned as a philosopher, sage, scribe, poet, astronomer, chief lector priest, magician, and architect (he designed and constructed the Step Pyramid at Sakkara, the world's first large, human-made stone structure). He was most famed as a physician and was probably responsible for the production of the seminal Ebers Papyrus, in which treatment for more than 700 diseases was detailed. He knew that the heart was the source of blood supply thousands of years before William Harvey rediscovered this principle and wrote about it in his *Exercitatio De Motu Cordis et Sanguinis in Animalibus*, published approximately 4,500 years after Imhotep's original discovery. Imhotep was deified in approximately 2850 B.C., and thus this great African physician, who was the first person to be known as a doctor throughout the world (20), came to be acknowledged as the god of medicine 50 centuries ago— almost 2,500 years before Aesculapius laid claim to the same title in Greece.

In the eighteenth century, a number of slaves contributed to medical science despite their bondage. Onesimus, a slave of Cotton Mather in Massachusetts, is credited with initiating the practice of smallpox inoculation, along with Dr. Zabdiel Boylston in Boston; Onesimus' work helped to stop the spread of smallpox in the American colonies in 1782, and it no doubt gave Jenner the idea for widespread vaccination that led to his fame.

James Derham of Philadelphia was a slave who bought his freedom with the proceeds from his successful medical practice. Papan, a Virginia slave, learned medicine from his masters and became so skilled at treating skin and venereal diseases that the Virginia legislature set him free. Cesar, a slave of South Carolina, was also set free because of his medical expertise. Primus was another "slave-doctor" and a pioneer in the treatment of rabies; when his master died, Primus took over his practice of surgery.

The earliest black physician in America was Lucas Santomee, who received his medical education in Holland and practiced in New York during the Colonial period. The first black graduate of a medical school was Dr. James McCune Smith, who graduated from Glasgow in 1837. The first black graduate of an American medical school was Dr. David John Peck (1847). The first black to be admitted to Harvard Medical School was Martin Robison Delaney in 1850. He did not graduate; he was blocked from attending classes by white students, and the school's administration, headed by Dean Oliver Wendell Holmes, cast him out along with two other blacks rather than defend his right to attend classes. He had attended for 2 years, and he obtained his medical doctorate later, through preceptorship training. In subsequent years, he served with distinction as a major in the Civil War.

Other notable early black doctors were Dr. John V. Degrasse, a graduate of Bowdoin College who studied medicine in Paris and was elected a member of the Massachusetts Medical Society; Dr. Peter W. Ray, born in approximately 1820, a Bowdoin graduate who practiced in New York City and became a member of the New York State Medical Society; Dr. Edwin C. Howard, born in 1846, who graduated from Harvard Medical School and later cofounded Mercy-Douglas Hospital in Philadelphia; Dr. Major R. Abbott, a graduate of Toronto University Medical School; and Dr. A. T. Augusta, an Army doctor who

FIG. 1-3. (*Clockwise from the upper left corner*) Dr. Martin Robison Delaney, Dr. John V. Degrasse, Dr. James McCune Smith, Dr. Major R. Abbott, Dr. Peter W. Ray, and Dr. Edwin C. Howard. (From Rogers JA. *Africa's gift to America.* New York: Futura Press, 1959:223, with permission.)

was given the responsibility of operating Freedman's Hospital as superintendent in the late 1860s (Fig. 1-3). Some other outstanding black doctors in medical history were Dr. Daniel Hale Williams, who performed the first operation on the living human heart in 1893 (Fig. 1-4); Dr. Charles R. Drew, who was head of the British blood plasma project for the army and conceived of the idea of the blood bank in 1941 (Fig. 1-5); and Dr. John Beauregard Johnson, chairman of medicine at Howard University of Medicine, who first called attention to the serious problem of hypertension in blacks (Fig. 1-6).

Medical education for blacks has been deficient in this country for centuries, and it remains so. At one time, after the Civil War, a number of black medical schools were opened specifically to train blacks to care for their own. By 1910, there were 11 of these schools. Nine were closed by 1920, however, after producing more than

FIG. 1-4. Daniel Hale Williams, M.D. (1858–1931). In 1893, he performed the first successful operation on the human heart, thus paving the way for the DeBakeys, Colleys, and Barnards of our day. *Schomburg Collection.* (From ref. 21, with permission.)

FIG. 1-5. Charles Richard Drew, M.D. (1904–1950). As head of the British blood plasma project in 1941, he conceived the idea of the blood bank and in so doing contributed to saving countless numbers of lives. *Schomburg Collection.* (From ref. 21, with permission.)

FIG. 1-6. John Beauregard Johnson, M.D. (1908–1972). His pioneering work on hypertension made him one of the few early exponents in this field. His warnings about the unrecognized dangers of this disease went unheeded until recently. *Schomburg Collection.* (From ref. 21, with permission.)

1,000 black physicians, because of criticism leveled against them by the famous Flexner Report on Medical Education in the United States and Canada. The Flexner Report was commissioned by the U.S. Government and authored by Dr. Abraham Flexner, a nonphysician; in his report, Dr. Flexner declared that only two of the schools should continue operations and indicated that these two should devote their efforts to producing "Negro sanitarians" instead of surgeons, because Negroes were a source of contagion and infections and were a threat to the health of whites. Except for the more recently organized programs at Morehouse in Atlanta and at Charles R. Drew University in Los Angeles, only Howard University in Washington, D.C., and Meharry in Nashville, Tennessee, have continued to be predominantly black medical schools to the present day.

BLACK-RELATED AND ETHNIC DISEASES

In 1975, I coined the term *black-related diseases* to cover conditions and diseases that seem to predominate in blacks (21). This concept forms a subgroup of the more comprehensive field of ethnic medicine, which involves the study of the broad distribution of diseases according to ethnic group, such as Tay-Sachs disease in Jews, thalassemia in peoples of Mediterranean origin, and nephrogenic diabetes insipidus in descendants of certain Ulster Scotsmen. Thus, black-related diseases represent only one aspect of the ethnic distribution of illnesses. Recognition that some diseases are peculiar to blacks must be understood within the context of the tendency for certain diseases to manifest themselves only in certain racial groups and that all racial groups display individual and characteristic reactions to the disease process.

Six categories of diseases and pathologic states are identified as black-related disease entities: congenital, genetic, environmental, infectious, oncogenic, and idiopathic. The main point to be made about these conditions, which are overwhelmingly due to environmental rather than genetic causes, is that definite illness can arise from being a black person in America. In this chapter, only a brief survey of black-related diseases can be provided. The reader is advised to consult reference 21 for further details.

Congenital Diseases

An example of a black-related condition in the congenital category is umbilical hernia, which is extremely common in black infants at birth. This congenital defect can lead to significant morbidity and even mortality secondary to hernial incarceration and strangulation and should by no means be lightly regarded. The cause for the increased incidence of umbilical hernia is unknown.

Genetic Diseases

The genetic category is best exemplified by sickle cell anemia, which is considered to be the prototype of all black-related diseases. More than 95% of persons with sickle cell anemia are black, although a wide variety of other ethnic groups have been involved. It is beyond the scope and purpose of this chapter to describe the clinical aspects of this condition in detail. However, it is important to point out that this most common of all recessive genetic diseases is still incurable and deserves continued attention from the medical profession as well as the public. More emphasis is now being properly placed on sickle cell trait, the heterozygous carrier state of sickle cell anemia, and until a cure can be found, control of the disease through education, testing, and counseling of carriers offers the greatest hope. This must be done in a very sensitive manner, with confidentiality receiving high priority.

Environmental Diseases

Hypertension is an example of an environmental disease. Although the exact sequence of events leading to the emergence of this disorder is unknown, it is believed that a large part of the causation is environmental. Hypertension qualifies as a black-related disease because it is much more prevalent among American blacks than among American whites (see Chapter 8). Programs that address the problem of hypertension in blacks must focus on social stress as a hypertension risk factor for blacks as well as on the judicious use of drug treatment.

Another environmental disease of great significance to blacks is lead poisoning. This condition is caused by poverty in almost every instance and is included as a black-related disease not because there is any influence of skin color on proneness to lead poisoning, but because blacks, as the largest and poorest racial minority in the United States, are more exposed to this health hazard. Lead intoxication is probably the most preventable of the major environmental diseases. It is estimated that hundreds of thousands of children are poisoned each year. Only a few effective screening programs exist in the United States, a situation that is nothing less than inexcusable. One wonders whether the allegedly higher prevalence of mental retardation among ethnic minorities as evidenced by performance in school may not be a manifestation of occult lead poisoning acquired in infancy that has progressed to the stage of encephalopathy.

Infectious Diseases

In the infectious disease category, rheumatic fever must be cited as the prototype of a disease that is still very important for blacks, although it is of diminished importance for whites. Rheumatic fever has experienced a steadily declining prevalence since 1900, which has prompted many public health officials to declare that it is no longer a problem. It is a disease of poverty much as lead poisoning is, however, and therefore it flourishes in the black ghetto. An interesting feature of this disease is that when groups of lower class blacks and whites are compared as to the prevalence of rheumatic fever, the former are found to be affected much more than the latter, probably because there is more overcrowding in the poor black community, thus facilitating the person-to-person transmission of the causative streptococcus. Clearly, here again the control of this serious disease depends on elimination of poverty and filth. The fact that most of the victims of rheumatic fever and its sequelae are black is a matter of circumstances (poverty, governmental neglect) rather than of race.

Oncogenic Diseases

Several disorders in the oncogenic (tumor-forming) category qualify as black related on the basis that their prevalence for blacks significantly exceeds that for whites, or because they show a relative increase in frequency for blacks while showing a decline for whites. Some of the most outstanding examples are cancers of the lung, esophagus, uterine cervix, stomach, and prostate gland. Too little emphasis has been placed on cancer control in the black community. This situation must change, and much more monetary consideration should be granted to the efforts against cancer in the black population.

Idiopathic Diseases

The final category, idiopathic (cause unknown) black-related disease, is exemplified by sarcoidosis, a granulomatous multisystem disease that affects blacks more commonly than whites by ratios ranging from 3:2 to 26:1. The typical patient with this disorder of unknown etiology is a young black woman with respiratory problems and chest pain. The illness may progress to serious complications and death, or it may be controlled by the early institution of appropriate therapy. Physicians who treat an inner-city clientele should be especially aware of sarcoidosis, which is a relatively common disease. No prevention and no cure have yet been developed, and emphasis must be placed on reducing the incidence of complications.

DISEASES TO WHICH BLACKS ARE RESISTANT

There are many diseases to which blacks manifest an unusual resistance, such as cystic fibrosis, phenylketonuria, hemophilia, and skin cancer. Whether there are innate protective mechanisms that render blacks almost immune to these disorders must be considered in the same manner as one considers why blacks are unusually susceptible to the black-related diseases described in the preceding sections. Certainly, no matter what the speculation, no one should presume from what has been presented that blacks are somehow superior or inferior to other racial groups. The intent of studying ethnic disease patterns is to discover information that will lead to improved medical treatment for minorities through concentrating on their special health characteristics.

CONCLUSIONS

As clinicians who should be concerned with providing the best possible care to our patients, we must acknowledge that black-related conditions and diseases exist so that we may contend with them. This means that consideration of the patient's race, ethnic group, and culture are of paramount importance in attempting to diagnose and manage diseases. We must also acknowledge that there is a difference in the way that certain ethnic and racial groups respond to certain drugs. This is seen in diseases such as hypertension, in which it is well known that blacks tend to respond suboptimally to particular drugs when compared to whites (22). The pharmaceutical industry now recognizes the significance of idiosyncratic drug responses in blacks and has launched a campaign to produce what might be called *designer drugs* for black patients (Fig. 1-7).

It should be clear that issues of race, ethnicity, culture, and religion have extremely important effects on health care. If we hope to improve medical care for those who are in greatest need, we must learn the principles that I have articulated and seek to use this knowledge in our contacts with patients. Be assured that doing so will result in improved health care for everyone.

——— IN DEVELOPMENT ———
NEW MEDICINES
——— FOR AFRICAN AMERICANS ———

Presented by the Pharmaceutical Manufacturers Association

1993 Survey
120 Medicines in Development for Diseases Of Major Concern to African Americans

The data show that African Americans have special health-care needs. For example:

• The death rate for cardiovascular disease is 39 percent higher for African American males than for white males, 68 percent higher for African American females than for white females.

• Although sickle cell disease does not exclusively affect African Americans, 99 percent of those who die from the disease are African Americans.

• The prevalence of diabetes is about 30 percent higher in African American adults than white adults.

America's pharmaceutical research industry is working to meet the special healthcare needs of African Americans. The Pharmaceutical Manufacturers Association (PMA) has found that 120 medicines are in development for diseases that disproportionately affect African Americans or are one of the top 10 causes of death for African Americans. (See "Facts about Diseases/Conditions Affecting African Americans" on page 9 for information about the social and economic impact of these diseases.)

An accompanying article by Richard A. Levy, Ph.D. (see page 17), emphasizes other reasons why the needs of all people—including all racial and ethnic minority groups—must be considered in discovering, developing and testing new drugs. Not all people respond in the same way to the same drug, and it is now clear that racial and ethnic factors may affect drug responses. Racial and ethnic differences may cause people to metabolize drugs differently, have different clinical responses and experience different side effects. For example, African American and white patients differ significantly in their responses to such heart drugs as beta-blockers, ACE inhibitors and diuretics.

All of the medicines listed in this report are in human clinical trials or are at the Food and Drug Administration for review.

Key findings of the survey include:

SUMMARY OF SURVEY RESULTS	1993
• Total Medicines in Development for African Americans	120
• Total Companies Developing Medicines for African Americans	50

SURVEY RESULTS BY DISEASE CATEGORY	1993
• AIDS/HIV Infection	21
• Blood Diseases	5
• Cancer	20
• Diabetes	14
• End-Stage Renal Disease	5
• Glaucoma	1
• Heart Disease/Hypertension	28
• Respiratory Disorders	25
• Stroke	7
• Tuberculosis	1

SURVEY RESULTS BY DEVELOPMENT STATUS	1993
• Phase I	23
• Phase I/II	7
• Phase II	41
• Phase II/III	5
• Phase III	45
• Phase I/II/III	1
• Phase Unspecified	3
• Applications Submitted	10

TOTAL RESEARCH PROJECTS	135
(reflects medicines in development for more than one use)	

• The four major categories of focus for research are heart disease with 28 medicines in development, respiratory disorders with 25, AIDS/HIV infection with 21, and cancer with 20.

• The three major causes of death among African Americans—heart disease, cancer and cerebrovascular disease—are the focus of 45 percent of the research projects represented in this survey report.

• Fourteen medicines are in development for diabetes, the fourth leading cause of death by disease among African Americans.

• Five medicines are in development for sickle cell disease.

• More than 40 percent of the research projects in this report are in their final stages of development.

• The 120 medicines in development involve 135 research projects

because some of the drugs are being tested for more than one use.

To identify the diseases covered by this survey, PMA worked with the International Coalition of Women Physicians, the National Association for the Advancement of Colored People, the National Association for Sickle Cell Disease, the National Medical Association, the National Black Child Development Institute and the National Black Nurses' Association. We thank these organizations and the other 53 cooperating organizations listed on the back page.

Gerald J. Mossinghoff
Gerald J. Mossinghoff
President
Pharmaceutical Manufacturers Association

FIG. 1-7. An example of the pharmaceutical industry's interest in diseases of blacks. (From the Pharmaceutical Manufacturers Association, Washington, D.C., 1993, with permission.)

REFERENCES

1. Watts ES. The biological race concept and disease of modern man. In: Rothschild HR, ed. *Biocultural aspects of disease*. New York: Academic Press, 1981:3–23.
2. *Webster's new twentieth century dictionary of the English language*, 2nd ed. New York: World Publishing Co., 1968.
3. Stanton W. *The leopard's spots: scientific attitudes toward race in America 1815–59*. Chicago: University of Chicago Press, 1960.
4. Stampp KM. *The peculiar institution. Slavery in the antebellum South*. New York: Vintage Books, 1956:8.
5. Weiss MM. The problem of angina pectoris in the Negro. *Am Heart J* 1939;17:711–715.
6. Becker LB, Han BH, Meyer PM, et al. Racial differences in the incidence of cardiac arrest and subsequent survival. *N Engl J Med* 1993;329:600–606.
7. Whittle J, Conigliaro J, Good CB, Lofgren RP. Racial differences in the use of invasive cardiovascular procedures in the Department of Veterans Affairs medical system. *N Engl J Med* 1993;329:621–627.
8. Simmons BE, Castener A, Santhanam V, et al. Outcome of coronary artery bypass grafting in black persons. *Am J Cardiol* 1987;59:547–551.
9. Castener A, Simmons BE, Mar M, Cooper R. Myocardial infarction among black patients: poor prognosis after hospital discharge. *Ann Intern Med* 1988;109:33–35.
10. Ayanian JZ. Heart disease in black and white. *N Engl J Med* 1993;329:656–658.
11. Montagu A. The concept of race. In: Montagu A, ed. *The concept of race*. Glenco, NY: Free Press, 1964:128.
12. Allport GW. *The nature of prejudice*. Cambridge, MA: Addison-Wesley Publishing Co., 1954.
13. Proctor R. *Racial hygiene: medicine under the Nazis*. Cambridge, MA: Harvard University Press, 1988.
14. Lifton RJ. *The Nazi doctors: medical killing and the psychology of genocide*. New York: Basic Books, 1986.
15. Müller-Hill B. *Murderous science: elimination by scientific selection of Jews, Gypsies, and others, Germany 1933–1945*. Oxford, New York: Oxford University Press, 1988.
16. Johnson KA. The color of health care. *Heart and Soul Magazine* 1994;Spring:51–57.
17. Fabrega H. Culture, biology, and the study of disease. In: Rothschild HR, ed. *Biocultural aspects of disease*. New York: Academic Press, 1981:54–92.
18. Boorstein DJ. *The discoverers*. New York: Random House, 1983:351–360.
19. Williams DR. Racism and health: a research agenda. *Ethn Dis* 1996;6:1–6.
20. Garrison FH. *An introduction to the history of medicine*. Philadelphia: WB Saunders, 1929.
21. Williams RA. *Textbook of black-related diseases*. New York: McGraw-Hill, 1975.
22. The sixth report of the Joint National Committee on the Prevention, Detection, Evaluation, and Treatment of High Blood Pressure. *Arch Intern Med* 1997;157:2433.

2

Molecular Genetics for the Clinical Cardiologist

Michael D. Schneider

Departments of Medicine, Cell Biology, and Molecular Biology and Biophysics,
Molecular Cardiology Unit, Baylor College of Medicine, Houston, Texas 77030

INTRODUCTION, VOCABULARY, AND CONCEPTS

Given the pronounced emphasis on often neglected social and economic issues in medical training and practice that distinguishes this First Symposium on Humane Medicine, one might ask whether molecular biology and genetics are actually relevant here, or whether they are, somehow, out of place—an embodiment of the venerable debates over nature versus nurture. One possible resolution to this presumed dichotomy is to point out that *all* diseases have a genetic basis, and yet *all* diseases have a social basis as well.

This may seem paradoxical to medical students and fellows, whose curriculum and skills lead them to focus most sharply on the individual patient's diagnosis and therapy. Trauma—for example, an auto accident—presents a simple counterexample: Where is the genetic component here? Where is the social component? To overlook the social dimension of this "straightforward" case is to neglect the large number of public decisions that contribute not only to the accident (e.g., the choice to fund roads instead of mass transit, the quality and clarity of road design, speed limits, seatbelt legislation, the crash-worthiness of vehicles) but also to subsequent events (e.g., community investment in emergency and paramedical services, geographic distribution of such services, the distance from the accident site to an appropriate health care facility, the quality and responsiveness of the available immediate and posthospitalization care).

On the other hand, overlooking the genetic dimension of trauma (and many seemingly straightforward disorders) means thinking about genetics only in terms of the mendelian inheritance of autosomal dominant, autosomal recessive, and sex-linked disease–determining genes, instead of recognizing that the capacity of organs, tissues, and cells to recover from injury is, ultimately, genetically determined. Which components of the body can restore damaged cells and structures and the efficiency of restoration are defined by genetic capabilities and limitations. This is why myocardial infarction and stroke are more devastating than injuries elsewhere—not merely because the heart and brain are more "essential" than other organs, but because their capacity to reconstitute cell number is lost, some say irreversibly, soon after birth.

I encourage the idea that, instead of viewing a genetic paradigm as an alternative to an environmental conception of disease, much can be gained by getting "under the hood," by seeking to understand the molecular underpinnings of garden-variety acquired diseases and ultimately exploiting this knowledge to provide a therapeutic benefit to patients. Before discussing specific examples of this principle (hereditary cardiomyopathies, congenital malformations of the heart and vasculature, restenosis after angioplasty, and myocardial infarction as a myocyte deficiency disease), a brief introduction of vocabulary and concepts is appropriate (1).

Gene Structure

In the cell nucleus, each chromosome comprises a linear array of genes, like beads on a string. Each gene itself comprises a linear array of deoxyribonucleotides (adenine, cytidine, guanine, and thymidine, the four chemical building blocks of DNA). DNA has two distinguishable functions in most genes: encoding proteins and directing the gene's expression. The double helix of DNA is two-stranded. Portions of one strand serve as a template that is transcribed into messenger RNA (a string of ribonucleic acids), which in turn travels to the ribosome as a template for encoding into protein [a string of amino acids (e.g., an enzyme or a structural component of the cell)]. The code for each amino acid resides in a three-base DNA or RNA triplet (codon). Each codon in messenger RNA binds to a complementary anticodon in a corresponding transfer RNA, adaptor molecules that shuttle the right amino acids to the nascent, elongating protein. Other classes of genes give rise to ribosomal RNA and transfer RNA. The number of possible codons is 64 ($4 \times 4 \times 4$), and of amino acids only 20; hence, many amino acids can have more than one codon. Specialized codons are the "start" codon (AUG), which encodes methionine (the first amino acid in each protein chain), and the "stop" codons (UAA, UGA, UAG), which signal the end of protein elongation.

Parts of the initially transcribed messenger RNA are edited out in a process known as *splicing*. Most often this process deletes blocks of noncoding RNA that do not correspond to amino acids of the eventual protein. In many cases, variable patterns of splicing are used to generate more than one protein from one gene. For instance, the multiple isoforms that exist for certain proteins may arise from multiple genes, from alternative splicing, or from a combination of the two. Portions of the DNA that correspond to portions of a final, processed messenger RNA are called *exons*. The intervening portions (which contain splicing signals and sometimes other regulatory cues but are otherwise poorly understood) are called *introns*. Messenger RNA also undergoes certain biochemical modifications after transcription, including the addition of a 3' polyadenylated "tail" and a 5' "cap," which are involved, respectively, in transportation of messenger RNA from the nucleus to the cytoplasm and the translation of messenger RNA into protein.

Gene Expression

Transcription of the gene to make RNA requires an RNA polymerase: In the construction of messenger RNA by protein-encoding genes, polymerase II is required.

This involves the physical binding or docking of polymerase to DNA near the starting point for transcription (usually at a T-A-T-A sequence called a *TATA box*). Whether the RNA polymerase can bind is controlled by a myriad of transcription factors, such as DNA-binding proteins that recognize specific DNA sequences or motifs and proteins that bind the DNA-binding proteins. Some transcription factors are ubiquitous and serve indispensably in the transcription of all genes (basal transcription factors). Other transcription factors are expressed only in some tissues, at certain ages, or in response to specific extracellular or environmental signals (mitogens, hormones, oxidative or ischemic stress, viral infection). Thus, genes get turned on only when their transcription factors are induced or when silent transcription factors become active (e.g., by protein phosphorylation, movement from the cytoplasm to the nucleus, or removal of an inhibitor). When silent transcription factors become active, cells of the organism express the right genes at the right time and place (hemoglobin in red blood cell progenitors, cardiac contractile proteins in ion channels in cardiac muscle, and so forth) and can adapt to circumstances by modulating, within limits, which genes are on or off. The regulatory regions of DNA that control gene expression, to which transcription factors bind, are referred to as *promoters* and *enhancers*. Promoters and enhancers are distinguished by position (promoters near the 5' start site for transcription, enhancers at sites farther upstream, sites inside the introns, or sites downstream from the 3' end of the gene), as well as by certain other operational differences.

Gene Defects

Errors in the DNA sequence (mutations) include the swapping of one nucleotide of DNA for another (substitution, or point mutation), the introduction of abnormal nucleotides (insertion), or the elimination of normal nucleotides (deletion). The colinear relationship of DNA to RNA to protein should make it clear that DNA mutations can have a direct effect on the resulting amino acid sequence and hence on protein function or stability. The effects are simplest in point mutations within exons. In insertion and deletion, if the length of the added or subtracted DNA segment is an integral multiple of three, amino acids lying downstream (farther toward the carboxyl-terminal end of the protein) are spared. However, if the length is not an exact multiple of three, all downstream codons are displaced by one or two and thus out of the normal reading frame for protein translation (frame-shift). Mutations affecting a protein's amino acid sequence are referred to as *missense mutations*; mutations creating a premature "stop" signal and an interruption of the protein are *nonsense mutations*. Because there may be several codons that indicate a particular amino acid, certain base changes do not affect the corresponding amino acid (silent mutations). Mutations also can occur within noncoding regions, and when this happens it can have dramatic, subtle, or no effects on the gene's expression.

Mutations in the germline occur with an estimated frequency of 1 in 1 million to 1 in 100,000 per locus per generation. Thus, when both parents have a normal genotype, inherited disease can arise *de novo*, a mechanism that explains some cases of sporadic hypertrophic cardiomyopathy. A polymorphism is by definition the existence of more than one gene sequence (allele) for a given locus, with a frequency in the population of less than 1%. It should not be forgotten that mutations also occur in somatic cells, are characteristic of most human cancers, and have long been postulated to occur in at least some atherosclerotic lesions. As genetic approaches are increasingly applied to complex multigenic disorders, such as hypertension or endemic forms of atherosclerosis, it is hoped that investigators will not neglect the opportunity to study the molecular basis for differences in prevalence, mechanism, and outcome in traditionally understudied populations.

GENETIC MANIPULATIONS: ANIMAL MODELS OF DISEASE

Much of the utility of molecular genetics in understanding cardiovascular disease, other aspects of medicine, and biology in general stems from its peculiar usefulness in answering questions of cause and effect, analogous to the role Koch's postulates played for infection (2). When expression of a given protein is increased in failing hearts or in atherosclerotic plaques, is this evidence of etiology, part of a countervailing negative feedback loop, or an innocent coincidence? Molecular genetics allows the researcher to influence and observe disease directly on the most basic level.

There are three methods by which molecular biologists can create a gain-of-function *in vivo* as a potential animal model of disease or as a test of a potential countermeasure: construction of transgenic animals (typically by DNA injection into the pronucleus of fertilized ova), DNA delivery (using naked DNA or lipid microdroplets—liposomes—as a vehicle), or viral delivery. Through these methods, a protein can be expressed at higher than normal levels, in a mutationally augmented form, or ectopically in the absence of normal expression.

Viral delivery most commonly makes use of retroviruses, adenoviruses, and adeno-associated viruses, which have complementary strengths and weaknesses. Retroviruses are useful when permanent gene transfer is desired (e.g., for the lifelong correction of hereditary defects in metabolism or immune function) because retroviruses insinuate their DNA into the host cell genome [although this insertion poses a potential risk (see the earlier discussion of insertional mutations)]. Retroviruses have a limited capacity that confines their usefulness to smaller exogenous genes, they do not infect nondividing cells as efficiently as other types of viruses and they are difficult to grow in the very high concentrations desirable for *in vivo* work. Adenoviruses have a large packaging capacity, they infect both proliferating and nondividing cells, they offer a minimal risk of insertional mutations, and they can readily be grown to high titers. For these reasons, recombinant adenoviruses are currently viewed as advantageous for gene therapy, although their usefulness is limited by the inflammatory responses raised against virus-infected cells and perhaps by the inherently limited duration of efficacy of nonchromosomal DNA. Adeno-associated viruses evoke a less inflammatory response, integrate into the host cell genome at a predetermined site, and are therefore likely to prove attractive as an alternative to the previously mentioned methods. Regardless of the viral vector used, one advantage of viral methods is their straightforward applicability, not only to rodents but also to larger mammals and to humans, as is discussed later.

The reciprocal strategy, loss-of-function, is also needed to prove causality. The principle here is to reduce or eliminate the protein's expression or, alternatively, its ability to function, to test what occurs in the partial or complete absence of the protein. Antisense reagents (oligonucleotides, or RNAs transcribed from the opposite DNA strand) can bind a messenger RNA, blocking its translation or causing its degradation or both. However, the specificity of antisense interventions has been questioned, and a "leaky" outcome is possible if the inhibition is incomplete. Dominant-inhibitory proteins are defective, nonfunctional mutations that override the activity of the normal (wild-type) endogenous protein when both are present—for example, in sequestration of or in competition for a substrate or other protein partner present in limited amounts. Insertional mutations, discussed earlier in connection with retroviruses, also occur when transgenic animals are made: The injected DNA is incorporated into chromosomal DNA in an uncontrolled way, usually but not always innocuously. Several intriguing mutations affecting heart formation have been identified in mice by fortuitous insertional mutations.

Saturation mutagenesis, or the intentional mutation of all genes, is not readily workable in mice and certainly not in larger mammals, but it has shed light on several of the earliest events for heart formation in flies and zebra fish. Given existing technologies, mice will offer a cardinal advantage in the ability to delete specific genes (knockout mutations) by replacing a gene segment with a defective one in primitive totipotent embryonal cells, injecting those cells into the blastocyst, confirming germline transmission in the progeny, and mating the defect to homozygosity. Because knockout mutations often result in embryonic or early postnatal lethality when an essential protein is disrupted, their use has been exceptionally informative for developmental biologists but can be problematic in the context of adult disease. For this reason, my collegues and I at Baylor and others have pursued technologies for a conditional knockout, limiting the gene deletion to the organ under study (e.g., the cardiac muscle, not all the cells of the body) or delaying the gene deletion until some outside trigger is introduced.

MOLECULAR GENETICS OF HEREDITARY CARDIAC HYPERTROPHY

One of the most dramatic illustrations of the insights achieved through the application of molecular genetics to cardiac disorders since the early 1990s has been the emerging concept of hypertrophic cardiomyopathy as a disease of the sarcomere. Although the clustering of hypertrophic cardiomyopathy in families had been appreciated earlier, identification of the disease gene(s) and proof of a genetic etiology required the advent of reverse genetics, also known as *positional cloning*. In positional cloning, mapping of the disease gene is based on its faithful coinheritance with nearby polymorphisms, instead of on individual testing to discern whether mutations might exist in a manageable number of pathophysiologically cogent candidate genes. (Polymorphisms on other chromosomes are coinherited only by chance. Polymorphisms on distant regions of the same chromosome are coinherited less than uniformly because of random crossing over and exchange of DNA between chromatids during meiosis.) Genes known to cause familial hypertrophic cardiomyopathy now include beta–myosin heavy chain (*beta-MHC*), alpha-tropomyosin, cardiac troponin T, myosin-binding protein C (*MyBP-C*), "essential" myosin light chain, "regulatory" myosin light chain, and cardiac troponin I, each coding for a protein of the sarcomere (3–6). Thus far, familial dilated cardiomyopathy has been ascribed to dystrophin (in Duchenne's or Becker's muscular dystrophy and X-linked cardiomyopathy) or to dystrophin-associated proteins (in limb-girdle dystrophy and hamster cardiomyopathy), suggesting that this disorder might involve proteins of the membrane-associated cytoskeleton (7). Other loci have been mapped for dilated cardiomyopathy, but the disease genes are not yet known.

MOLECULAR GENETICS OF ACQUIRED CARDIAC HYPERTROPHY

How does the discovery of an etiologic gene, such as *beta-MHC* mutations in familial hypertrophic cardiomyopathy, relate to less esoteric forms of acquired cardiac hypertrophy such as hypertension, aortic valve disease, or aortic coarctation? A central concern for many investigators has been the exact molecular events that couple mechanical load to long-term changes in cardiac growth (analogous, perhaps, to the relation between neural activity and long-term memory). Although the existence of the mechanical sensor that detects the change in wall stress is unproved, much more has been learned of the subsequent signal transduction events in pressure-overload hypertrophy (mechanical stress in passively stretched cardiac muscle cells). These include the activation of a plethora of cytoplasmic signaling cascades, including multiple protein kinase families (8). Even more important, perhaps, there now is recognition that "hypertrophy" entails more than an overall increase in heart mass and myocyte size. It is understood that hypertrophy is typically associated with changes in the expression of an astonishing number of cardiac genes, sometimes referred to as *activation of a fetal phenotype* (9).

The first changes to be identified include isoforms of myosin heavy and light chains, isoforms of actin, and natriuretic factors, accompanied by down-regulation of the calcium pump in sarcoplasmic reticulum. One potential cascade that might explain this complex spectrum of changes is suggested by the up-regulation of certain protooncogenes (myc, fos, jun) and other immediate-early, rapidly responsive transcription factors, which appear, from gene delivery experiments in cultured cells, to be partly responsible for the events that follow. Mechanical load also results in the up-regulation of multiple intramyocardial growth factors, including transforming growth factor–beta, fibroblast growth factors, insulin-like growth factor I, vascular endothelial growth factor, tumor necrosis factor–alpha, and others. Because many of these proteins can elicit the fetal phenotype or hypertrophic growth of cardiac muscle in culture, autocrine and paracrine mechanisms may be in play during myocardial hypertrophy. Transgenic models and other genetic methods discussed above have begun to be applied to these postulated mediators *in vivo*. In part because fetal gene induction has been observed in human hypertrophic cardiomyopathy, and because the disease arises exclusively from sarcomeric proteins (not conventionally regarded as regulators of cell growth), the functional connection between sarcomeric gene mutations and hypertrophy per se is widely thought to involve direct effects on sarcomeric function and indirect effects on wall stress. Ultimately, the same cascade is engaged for cardiac hypertrophy as for hypertension or other extrinsic loads.

MOLECULAR GENETICS OF CONGENITAL HEART DISEASE

Until recently, elucidating a molecular basis for congenital heart malformations might have been viewed as intractably complex (10–12). However, noteworthy illustrations of success include supravalvular aortic stenosis (elastin), Marfan syndrome (fibrillin 1), Holt-Oram syndrome (the "T-box" transcription factor, TBX5), velocardiofacial and DiGeorge syndromes (chromosome 22 deletions), and autosomal recessive heterotaxy (connexin 43). Saturation mutagenesis in flies has disclosed novel genes controlling heart formation, such as *tinman*, named for the heart-deficient woodsman in *The Wizard of Oz*. The existence (and functional importance) of homologous genes in vertebrates is already apparent. Saturation mutagenesis in zebra fish has pointed to literally dozens of loci controlling heart morphogenesis, although in this species a sufficiently precise positional map of the genome is still in progress, and cloning the etiologic genes remains to be accomplished.

REENGINEERING THE CARDIOVASCULAR SYSTEM: GENE-BASED THERAPIES FOR CARDIOVASCULAR DISEASE

As hinted at earlier, a substantial part of the excitement concerning novel technologies for gene delivery is the prospect that such approaches might be used to achieve clinical objectives—to empower cells to make proteins they lack, for example, or to block the expression or action of disease-causing genes (13). In cardiovascular medicine, the likeliest scenarios for early implementation include gene therapies for lipid reduction, restenosis, and angiogenesis. Human clinical trials are in progress for each of these.

Lipid Reduction

Because defects or deficiencies in the low-density lipoprotein (LDL) receptor are a hallmark of familial hypercholesterolemia, gene rescue in this setting has convincing and cogent appeal in that it involves the use of somatic cell gene therapy to correct the defect by upregulating the receptors, thus "rescuing" the patient (14). More speculative is the long-term benefit of augmenting levels of this receptor compared to the long-term effects of statins in patients with increased LDL but no receptor defect. Other candidate genes for lipid reduction therapy that are protective in transgenic animals include lecithin:cholesterol acyltransferase (15) and apolipoprotein E (16). Like the correction of other disorders of metabolism, gene therapy for lipid reduction offers certain attractions. The lifelong nature of the disease justifies a gene-based approach as an alternative to decades of pharmaceuticals. The site and uniformity of gene delivery are not critical. Moreover, the liver is a readily accessible target, absorbing virus with extraordinary efficiency even after intravenous injections.

Restenosis

A large number of gene-based interventions have already been applied investigationally to restenosis after angioplasty and the related issue of intimal proliferation after saphenous vein grafting. The very high prevalence with which angioplasty subsequently fails, the predictable and early time frame in which restenosis occurs, and, from a technical point of view, the remarkable access provided to the coronary anatomy at the time of catheterization, angioplasty, or graft placement all favor this intensive effort. Multiple mitogens exist in serum or in the vessel wall as potential agents driving restenosis. The relative importance of these is conjectural; animal studies with inhibitors of one or the other are inconclusive, and as-yet-unidentified mitogens might plausibly be involved. It is therefore logical that much of the effort has focused on the cell's machinery for cell cycle control, which appears to operate as a final common pathway for all mitogens studied thus far.

Cell proliferation depends on five multigene families: cell cycle–dependent proteins called *cyclins*; the cyclin-dependent protein kinases (Cdks); Cdk inhibitors; Rb and related pocket proteins, which are the targets of the Cdks; and E2F transcription factors, whose release from pocket proteins activates E2F-dependent genes necessary for DNA synthesis (among them the mitotic Cdk, Cdc2, and proliferating cell nuclear antigen). Potential interventions for intimal hyperplasia after restenosis or grafting encompass each of these levels and include mitogen-binding proteins to block receptor binding, dominant-negative mitogen receptors, dominant-negative signaling proteins such as Ras (17), Cdk inhibitors (18), nonphosphorylatable Rb (19), a DNA decoy for E2F (20) (double-stranded oligonucleotides corresponding to the E2F binding site in E2F-dependent genes), and antisense reduction of Cdc2 and proliferating cell nuclear antigen (21). In contrast with each of these approaches aimed at growth arrest is an approach derived from cancer gene therapy (herpes simplex virus thymidine kinase with the drug ganciclovir) to kill cells that express the exogenous enzyme (22).

Angiogenesis

Angioplasty, stents, and surgical revascularization are each aimed at restoring blood flow to the distal circulation but are limited by certain anatomic requirements. The theoretic possibility of using hormone-like peptides (growth factors) selectively to promote vessel growth in ischemic tissues is encouraged by the explosive growth of new information (including new factors) from studies of tumor angiogenesis and development. Recombinant proteins and plasmids or viruses encoding the proteins are testable for this form of therapy. Vascular endothelial growth factor has the advantage of being highly selective for endothelial cells and thus unlikely to have undesired consequences for other cell types (23). Fibroblast growth factors (FGFs) can also promote angiogenesis, and at least three members of the family (FGF-1, FGF-2, and

FGF-5) have been shown to promote blood flow in the heart (24–26). Because FGFs also affect vessel tone (27), great caution is advisable in assessing the claims made for this family; increased blood flow and blood vessel formation are hardly synonymous.

Myocardial Infarction as a Myocyte-Deficiency Disease

The clinical hook in our laboratories at Baylor concerns a related problem in defective growth. From one point of view, the problem with infarction is not that ventricular muscle cells die but that they lack the ability to restore cell number, having lost the capacity for proliferative growth soon after birth (the postmitotic phenotype). The need to restore myocyte number also is apparent in end-stage heart failure, in which cell dropout due to cell suicide (apoptosis) has been implicated. Thus, genes controlling cardiac myocyte proliferation and death have been identified as potential novel targets for heart failure therapy (28). It is noteworthy (looking back on the cascade for mitogenic signaling discussed under Restenosis) that cyclins and Cdks are down-regulated markedly in adult myocardium, whereas several Cdk inhibitors are markedly up-regulated. Our approach to overriding the molecular constraints that block proliferation in adult ventricular muscle cells has been to bypass the mitogen receptors, mitogenic signaling cascades, regulators of pocket protein phosphorylation, and pocket proteins themselves by viral gene transfer, using the adenoviral protein E1A (which binds and inactivates the pocket, releasing E2F) or exogenous E2F-1 (29–31). These experiments have confirmed the existence of a pocket protein–dependent pathway for growth arrest in cardiac muscle and of a second pathway via other cell cycle regulators. These studies have substantiated the ability to restart the cell cycle and double DNA content, even in adult ventricular muscle cells *in vivo*, by viral delivery of genes to cardiac muscle cells in tissue culture and by direct injection to the intact adult myocardium. These interventions have unmasked a second block, at the completion of DNA synthesis (the G2/M checkpoint), which prevents the muscle cells from progressing to mitosis. Because forced cell cycle reentry was accompanied by apoptosis, these investigations also led to the finding that particular antiapoptotic genes could be used to block cell death in this setting and conceivably in apoptosis caused by pathophysiologic triggers. Novel means for deleting genes only from the heart, allowing the remainder of the body to develop and function normally, may prove useful in deciphering the complexities of cardiac growth control, as well as proteins' other essential functions in the heart (32). Questions that remain unanswered include whether relief of cell death via antiapoptotic genes affects the outcome of ischemic injury or reoxygenation, whether mitosis can be evoked in postmitotic cells by interventions aimed at Cdc2 or other proteins active in the G2/M transition, and which endogenous proteins actually impose the quasiirreversible lock on cycling in adult ventricular muscle.

REFERENCES

1. Alberts B, Bray B, Lewis J, Raff M. *Molecular biology of the cell.* New York: Garland, 1995.
2. Chien KR. Genes and physiology: molecular physiology in genetically engineered animals. *J Clin Invest* 1996;97:901–909.

3. Geisterfer-Lowrance AA, Kass S, Tanigawa G, et al. A molecular basis for familial hypertrophic cardiomyopathy: a beta cardiac myosin heavy chain gene missense mutation. *Cell* 1990;62:999–1006.
4. Thierfelder L, Watkins H, MacRae C, et al. Alpha-tropomyosin and cardiac troponin T mutations cause familial hypertrophic cardiomyopathy: a disease of the sarcomere. *Cell* 1994;77:701–712.
5. Bonne G, Carrier L, Bercovici J, et al. Cardiac myosin binding protein-C gene splice acceptor site mutation is associated with familial hypertrophic cardiomyopathy. *Nat Genet* 1995;11:438–440.
6. Poetter K, Jiang H, Hassanzadeh S, et al. Mutations in either the essential or regulatory light chains of myosin are associated with a rare myopathy in human heart and skeletal muscle. *Nat Genet* 1996;13:63–69.
7. Cox GF, Kunkel LM. Dystrophies and heart disease. *Curr Opin Cardiol* 1997;12:329–343.
8. Yamazaki T, Komuro I, Yazaki Y. Molecular mechanism of cardiac cellular hypertrophy by mechanical stress. *J Mol Cell Cardiol* 1995;27:133–140.
9. Parker TG, Schneider MD. Growth factors, proto-oncogenes, and plasticity of the cardiac phenotype. *Annu Rev Physiol* 1991;53:179–200.
10. Payne RM, Johnson MC, Grant JW, Strauss AW. Toward a molecular understanding of congenital heart disease. *Circulation* 1995;91:494–504.
11. Olson EN, Srivastava D. Molecular pathways controlling heart development. *Science* 1996;272:671–676.
12. Fishman MC, Chien KR. Fashioning the vertebrate heart: earliest embryonic decisions. *Development* 1997;124:2099–2117.
13. Nabel EG. Gene therapy for cardiovascular disease. *Circulation* 1995;91:541–548.
14. Kozarsky KF, Jooss K, Donahee M, Strauss JF, Wilson JM. Effective treatment of familial hypercholesterolaemia in the mouse model using adenovirus-mediated transfer of the VLDL receptor gene. *Nat Genet* 1996;13:54–62.
15. Berard AM, Foger B, Remaley A. High plasma HDL concentrations associated with enhanced atherosclerosis in transgenic mice overexpressing lecithin:cholesteryl acyltransferase. *Nat Med* 1997;3:744–749.
16. Kashyap VS, Santamarinafojo S, Brown DR. Apolipoprotein E deficiency in mice: gene replacement and prevention of atherosclerosis using adenovirus vectors. *J Clin Invest* 1995;96:1612–1620.
17. Ueno H, Yamamoto H, Ito SI, Li JJ, Takeshita A. Adenovirus-mediated transfer of a dominant-negative H-ras suppresses neointimal formation in balloon-injured arteries in vivo. *Arterioscler Thromb Vasc Biol* 1997;17:898–904.
18. Yang ZY, Simari RD, Perkins ND, et al. Role of the p21 cyclin-dependent kinase inhibitor in limiting intimal cell proliferation in response to arterial injury. *Proc Natl Acad Sci U S A* 1996;93:7905–7910.
19. Chang MW, Barr E, Seltzer J, et al. Cytostatic gene therapy for vascular proliferative disorders with a constitutively active form of the retinoblastoma gene product. *Science* 1995;267:518–522.
20. Morishita R, Gibbons GH, Horiuchi M. A gene therapy strategy using a transcription factor decoy of the E2F binding site inhibits smooth muscle proliferation in vivo. *Proc Natl Acad Sci U S A* 1995;92:5855–5859.
21. Mann MJ, Gibbons GH, Tsao PS, et al. Cell cycle inhibition preserves endothelial function in genetically engineered rabbit vein grafts. *J Clin Invest* 1997;99:1295–1301.
22. Simari RD, San H, Rekhter M. Regulation of cellular proliferation and intimal formation following balloon injury in atherosclerotic rabbit arteries. *J Clin Invest* 1996;98:225–235.
23. Tsurumi Y, Kearney M, Chen DF. Treatment of acute limb ischemia by intramuscular injection of vascular endothelial growth factor gene. *Circulation* 1997;96:382–388.
24. Unger EF, Banai S, Shou MT. Basic fibroblast growth factor enhances myocardial collateral flow in a canine model. *Am J Physiol* 1994;266:H1588–H1595.
25. Giordano FJ, Ping PP, McKirnan MD. Intracoronary gene transfer of fibroblast growth factor-5 increases blood flow and contractile function in an ischemic region of the heart. *Nat Med* 1996;2:534–539.
26. Schumacher B, Pecher P, von Specht BU, Stegmann T. Induction of neoangiogenesis in ischemic myocardium by human growth factors. *Circulation* 1998;97:645–650.
27. Zhou M, Sutliff RL, Paul RJ, et al. Fibroblast growth factor 2 control of vascular tone. *Nat Med* 1998;4:201–207.
28. Cohn JN, Bristow MR, Chien KR, et al. Report of the National Heart, Lung, and Blood Institute Special Emphasis Panel on Heart Failure Research. *Circulation* 1997;95:766–770.

29. Kirshenbaum LA, Abdellatif M, Chakraborty S, Schneider MD. Human E2F-1 reactivates cell cycle progression in ventricular myocytes and represses cardiac gene transcription. *Dev Biol* 1996;179: 402–411.
30. Kirshenbaum LA, Schneider MD. Adenovirus E1A represses cardiac gene transcription and reactivates DNA synthesis in ventricular myocytes, via alternative pocket protein and p300-binding domains. *J Biol Chem* 1995;270:7791–7794.
31. Agah R, Kirshenbaum LA, Truong LD, et al. Adenoviral delivery of E2F-1 directs cell cycle re-entry and p53-independent apoptosis in post-mitotic adult myocardium in vivo. *J Clin Invest* 1997;100: 2722–2728.
32. Agah R, Frenkel PA, French BA, Michael LH, Overbeek PA, Schneider MD. Gene recombination in postmitotic cells: targeted expression of Cre recombinase provokes cardiac-restricted, site-specific rearrangement in adult ventricular muscle in vivo. *J Clin Invest* 1997;100:169–179.

3

A Biopsychosocial Perspective: Socioeconomic Influences on Health*

Norman B. Anderson

Office of Behavioral and Social Sciences Research, Office of the Director, National Institutes of Health, Bethesda, Maryland 20892, Departments of Psychology and Psychiatry, Duke University, Durham, North Carolina 27710, and Society of Behavioral Medicine, Bethesda, Maryland 20814

It was a pleasure for me to participate in the first Symposium on Humane Medicine. As the first Associate Director of the National Institutes of Health (NIH) for Behavioral and Social Sciences Research, I believe the theme of this conference is congruous with many of my goals and objectives at the NIH. In this paper, four topics are addressed. First, the paper provides a brief overview of the goals and activities of the Office of Behavioral and Social Sciences Research (OBSSR) at the NIH, with a focus on a biopsychosocial perspective of the determinants of health. Next, as an example of biopsychosocial influences on health, the paper summarizes research on lower socioeconomic status (SES), a major risk factor for illness and death in our society. Some of the reasons for the association between SES and health are discussed, with a special focus on the black population. Finally, the paper describes some of the clinical implications of a biopsychosocial perspective on health.

The OBSSR was created by the U.S. Congress in 1993 to enhance the NIH's research efforts in the behavioral and social sciences. The creation of the OBSSR was in part an acknowledgment that behavioral and social factors not only are significant contributors to health and illness but frequently interact with biological factors to influence health outcomes. In addition, it was recognized that behavioral and social factors represent important avenues for treatment and prevention.

The guiding philosophy of OBSSR is that scientific advances in the understanding, treatment, and prevention of disease will be accelerated by greater attention to the full range of factors that determine health outcomes—behavioral, sociocultural, environmental, physiologic, and genetic—and the interactions between them (Fig. 3-1) (1). Although the contribution of each category may vary

---

*The views expressed herein are not necessarily those of the National Institutes of Health or the U.S. Department of Health and Human Services.

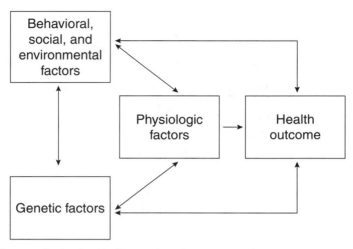

FIG. 3-1. Factors affecting health. (From ref. 4, with permission.)

from disease to disease, there is now ample evidence supporting an integrated or biopsychosocial perspective on causation for most health problems. This perspective may be applied to an array of disorders, including heart disease, cancer, diabetes, acquired immunodeficiency syndrome, depression, substance abuse, stroke, asthma, injuries, anxiety disorders, chronic pain, infant mortality, and dental problems (for examples, see references 2,3).

BIOPSYCHOSOCIAL INFLUENCES ON HEALTH: THE EXAMPLE OF SOCIOECONOMIC STATUS

One of the clearest examples of the importance of psychosocial and behavioral influences on health is the effect of SES. Anderson and Armstead provide a representation of the association between SES and health in developed countries (Fig. 3-2) (4). As SES rises, morbidity and mortality rates generally fall. This inverse relationship is observed whether SES is measured by education, income, or occupation and does not appear to reflect the drifting down through the SES hierarchy of individuals with serious physical illnesses (5,6). The SES-health gradient extends to a wide array of health problems (7) and may predict prognosis after illness is present (8,9). For more detailed information on specific studies of SES and health, several excellent reviews are available (10–12).

Perhaps the most pressing question for health researchers is how SES influences health outcomes, or how it "gets under the skin." Anderson and Armstead (4) describe six categories of variables that might participate in the linkage between SES and health (Table 3-1). These include sociodemographic; economic; social, environmental, and medical; behavioral and psychological; physiologic; and health outcome

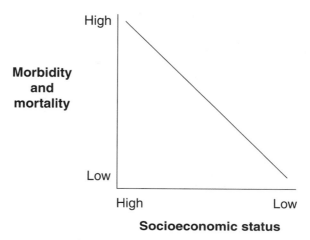

FIG. 3-2. Representation of the relationship between socioeconomic status and health outcomes.

variables. Although this diagram conveniently illustrates the many factors that may be involved in the link between SES and health, it does not truly capture the number and complexity of the interactions that may occur within and across categories. Using the literature on ethnic group differences in health, however, I provide illustrative examples of some of these interactions.

It is frequently assumed that SES differences in access to health care (see Table 3-1, third column) can account for SES differences in health outcomes. Although universal health care coverage is critically important, its initiation will probably not level out the SES-health gradient. According to Adler et al. (10), this is true for at least three reasons. First, countries that have universal health insurance show approximately the same SES-health gradient as that found in the United States, where such insurance is not provided. Second, SES differences in health outcomes can be found even in the upper ranges of the SES hierarchy, where health insurance coverage is closer to universal. Third, SES differences appear in patients with diseases that are not amenable to treatment (e.g., some types of cancer), as well as in patients with diseases that are. It seems, therefore, that even after the implementation of much-needed health care reform in the United States, the SES-health gradient will more than likely persist.

Ethnicity, Socioeconomic Status, and Health

It is well known that ethnicity influences SES in the United States. For example, blacks have a significantly lower SES than whites by every measure (13,14). What is not often recognized, however, is that morbidity and mortality rates are higher for blacks than for whites at most levels of SES. Using data from the 1986 National Health Interview Survey, Pappas et al. (15) reported that, even given the same educational attainment, mortality rates are higher among black men and women than in

TABLE 3-1. *Possible factors linking socioeconomic factors and health*

Socio-demographic	Socioeconomic status	Social, environmental, and medical	Psychological and behavioral	Physiologic	Outcomes
Age	Education	Residential	Psychological	Genetics	Health and
Ethnicity	Income	characteristics	distress	Cardio-	illness
Gender	Occupation	Occupational	Personality	vascular	
Location	Family wealth	environment	factors	Immune	
	Perceived	Social support	Health-promoting	Muscular	
	socioeco-	Social/profes-	behaviors	Endocrine	
	nomic status	sional hier-	Health-damaging	Renal	
	Economic	archy	behaviors	Weight	
	mobility	Access to health		Height	
	Childhood socio-	care			
	economic				
	status				
	Material pos-				
	sessions				
	Trading/				
	bartering				
	practices				
	National income				
	distribution				

From ref. 15, with permission.

whites (Figs. 3-3 and 3-4). The disparity between blacks and whites is especially striking at the low end of the SES hierarchy.

These data are particularly relevant given that differences in health between blacks and whites are often attributed to group differences in SES. That is, it is assumed that if blacks and whites were matched in SES, group differences in health would be eliminated or at least substantially reduced. Some research indicates that ethnic group differences in SES can account for group differences in some health outcomes (6,16); yet the data from Pappas et al. (15) suggest that the issue may be more complex than is generally acknowledged. There is also the important possibility that the nature and experience of SES is different for each ethnic group. If this is so, research designed to understand the processes responsible for the SES-health gradient should be ethnic-group specific and should not stop at explaining group differences. This issue is addressed in the following sections.

Ethnicity, Socioeconomic Status, and Environmental Exposures

Clear relationships have been found between ethnicity, SES, and residential, social, and occupational environments (see Table 3-1, third column). William Wilson (17) showed that poverty is associated with different residential environments in blacks than it is in whites. Wilson found that among residents of the five largest cities in the United States in 1980, 68% of all poor whites lived in census-defined non-

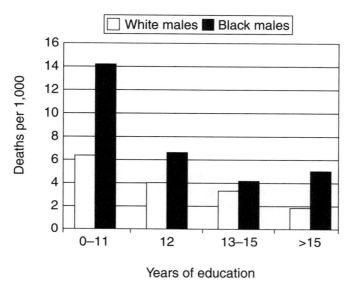

FIG. 3-3. Mortality rates in males by ethnicity and education. (From ref. 15, with permission.)

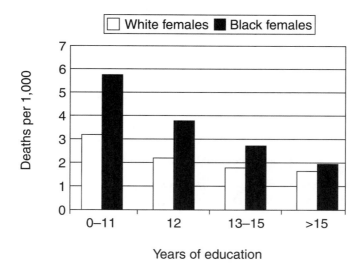

FIG. 3-4. Mortality rates in females by ethnicity and education. (Adapted from ref. 15.)

poverty areas, whereas only 15% of poor blacks and 20% of poor Hispanics lived in nonpoverty areas. Furthermore, whereas only 7% of poor whites lived in extreme poverty areas, 39% of all poor blacks and 32% of all poor Hispanics lived in extreme poverty areas. Wilson's findings are important from a health perspective because other research indicates that living in impoverished environments increases risk for all-cause mortality, independent of other risk factors (18). That is, persons who live in neighborhoods where a high percentage of their neighbors are poor are at greater risk of death from all causes, independent of their individual SES. Thus, it is possible that group differences in residential environments could partially explain the disparity in health outcomes between poor blacks and poor whites.

Furthermore, potentially health-protective social relationships (19) may occur less often in high-poverty environments. Compared to blacks living in nonpoverty areas, those residing in high-poverty areas have a higher percentage of individuals who report being unmarried, having no current partner, and having no best friend. Blacks in general, but especially low-income blacks, are disproportionately exposed to hazardous waste facilities and uncontrolled toxic waste sites (20).

Ethnicity, Socioeconomic Status, and Psychological and Behavioral Factors

Relatively little research has examined the interactions of ethnicity, SES, and psychological and behavioral factors related to health. Studies of ethnic differences in health behavior frequently statistically control for SES, instead of examining its interaction with ethnicity. The findings of studies that have looked at these interactions suggest that blacks with lower SES have a higher risk profile than other groups, which may account for their higher mortality rate.

Kessler and Neighbors (21) found that blacks with low SES reported more stress in their lives than did whites with low SES and upper-income blacks. Some epidemiologic studies have documented a higher prevalence of smoking among black adults, especially among low-income blacks, who are at the greatest risk for lung cancer and heart disease (22).

Ethnicity, Socioeconomic Status, and Physiologic Processes

Although black-white differences have been observed in a number of physiologic variables, few studies have examined the interaction of these variables with SES and ethnicity. The one exception is obesity, in which black women have been shown to have a higher prevalence during their adult years than black men, white women, and white men. The prevalence of obesity in black women is higher at every level of SES than it is in white women, but this is particularly true among persons with lower SES (23,24).

Given the differences in the nature and experience of SES in blacks and whites, future research should focus more carefully on how SES might be influencing health outcomes differently in each group. In addition, the effects of SES on behavioral and psychosocial functioning should be explored in other cultural groups, including Asian-Americans, Latin Americans, and Native Americans.

IMPLICATIONS OF THE BIOPSYCHOSOCIAL PERSPECTIVE
FOR HEALTH CARE PRACTICE

As illustrated in Fig. 3-1, the essence of humane medicine is in part the recognition that the illnesses presented by patients are due to dynamic interactions between biological, social, behavioral, and psychological factors. In addition to representing the factors affecting health, Fig. 3-1 also highlights possible targets for intervention. Most of modern medicine focuses on interventions aimed at the pathophysiology via drug treatments. There is now some indication that discoveries in genetics research will lead to effective gene therapies. The extensive literature on successful behavioral interventions that have been demonstrated to help with an array of health problems should also be considered. Some of this research is summarized here.

Behavioral Interventions

Behavioral interventions, also known as *mind/body* or *behavioral medicine* interventions, are those that provide patients with the skills and knowledge they need to manage or prevent illnesses. Behavioral approaches may be used as preventive interventions for the reduction of risk factors, such as smoking, or to alleviate physical symptoms or pathophysiologic conditions associated with chronic diseases. Behavioral approaches have been used successfully to treat such chronic illnesses as arthritis, hypertension, asthma, chronic pain, coronary heart disease, depression, cancer, and diabetes. Specific approaches include goal setting, problem solving, self-monitoring, cognitive therapy, health education, relaxation training, support groups, and exercise.

For example, stress management techniques involving relaxation training and cognitive therapy (i.e., teaching patients to alter stress-producing thought patterns) have been shown to prevent recurrent cardiac events in patients with a history of heart disease (25). These treatments also show efficacy in reducing chronic pain caused by a variety of medical conditions (26). Supportive group therapy with cancer patients has been shown to improve mood, ease adjustment, and alleviate pain, and randomized trials indicate that those who participated in these groups had a significantly longer life expectancy than those who did not (27,28). Stress management strategies such as transcendental meditation have successfully reduced blood pressure in blacks with hypertension (29,30). Self-management approaches involving health education, problem solving, cognitive therapy, skill development, and self-monitoring have been demonstrated to improve knowledge, self-care behaviors, and metabolic control in patients with diabetes (31–33).

Behavioral interventions are not only useful in altering symptoms and pathophysiologic conditions but may also result in decreased health care use and costs. The use and cost of health care have both been reduced through behavioral interventions in populations such as frequent users of Medicaid services (34), arthritis patients (35), chronic pain patients (36), and children with fevers (37). These approaches have also reduced hospital stays after surgery (38) and improved pregnancy outcomes, as evidenced by fewer cesarean sections, shorter labor, and fewer neonatal complications (39,40).

Behavioral interventions can also help alter health-damaging behaviors such as smoking, alcohol abuse, physical inactivity, improper diet, and medication nonadherence. For example, behavioral research suggests that smoking cessation is best characterized as a process, with smokers moving between different stages of readiness to quit, from being uninterested in quitting to considering the possibility of quitting, to attempting to quit, and finally to maintaining smoking abstinence (41). Based on these stages of smoking cessation, an intervention was developed to aid physicians in helping patients move through the quitting process. The intervention involves *asking* patients about smoking habits, *advising* them to quit, *assisting* those who want to stop, and *arranging* follow-up visits. Similarly, research has indicated that physicians can significantly improve adherence to medication regimens by

- Using simple, clear instructions
- Using short words and sentences
- Providing written instruction
- Having patients repeat instructions
- Discussing potential barriers to adherence
- Tailoring the regimen for the patient's schedule and lifestyle
- Suggesting the use of reminder cues at home
- Using telephone follow-up and verbal reinforcement

Despite the overwhelming evidence in support of a biopsychosocial perspective on health, most medical schools in the United States do not offer training in behavioral approaches to treatment and prevention. However, opportunities for continuing education in these treatments are available from a number of scientific societies. These include the Society of Behavioral Medicine, the Association for Advancement of Behavior Therapy, and the Society for Public Health Education. At the very least, physicians should recognize that behavioral treatments are valuable options for interventions and be prepared to refer patients to appropriate professionals offering these approaches (e.g., psychologists, psychiatric social workers or nurses, psychiatrists). In addition, many community-based organizations offer classes on such topics as stress management, exercise, or smoking cessation at no or very low cost. Physicians should strongly recommend participation in these programs for patients who might benefit from them. Whether making a referral to another professional or directing patients to community-based programs, physicians should routinely follow up with patients to ensure that recommendations have been followed or to provide additional encouragement when recommendations have not been followed.

REFERENCES

1. Office of Behavioral and Social Sciences Research. A strategic plan for the Office of Behavioral and Social Sciences Research at the National Institutes of Health. NIH Publication no. 97–4237. Washington, D.C.: National Institutes of Health.

2. Anderson NB. Levels of analysis in health science: a framework for integrating sociobehavioral and biomedical research. *Ann N Y Acad Sci* (*in press*).
3. Friedman R, Sobel D, Myers P, Caudill M, Benson H. Behavioral medicine, clinical health psychology, and cost offset. *Health Psychol* 1995;14:509–518.
4. Anderson NB, Armstead CA. Toward understanding the association of socioeconomic status and health: a new challenge for the biopsychosocial approach. *Psychosom Med* 1995;57:213–225.
5. Fox AJ, Goldblatt P, Jones D. Social class mortality differentials: artefact, selection or life circumstance. *J Epidemiol Community Health* 1985;39:1–8.
6. Haan MN, Kaplan GA, Syme SL. Socioeconomic status and health: old observations and new thoughts. In: Bunker J, Gomby D, Kehrer B, eds. *Pathways to health: the role of social factors.* Menlo Park, CA: Henry H. Kaiser Family Foundation, 1989:76–135.
7. Pincus T, Kallahan L, Burkhauser R. Most chronic diseases are reported more frequently by individuals with fewer than 12 years of formal education in the ages 18–64 in the United States population. *J Chronic Dis* 1987;40:865–874.
8. Williams RB, Barefoot JC, Kaliff RM, et al. Prognostic significance of social and economic resources among medically treated patients with angiographically documented coronary artery disease. *JAMA* 1992;267:520–524.
9. Ruberman W, Weinblatt E, Goldberg JD, et al. Psychosocial influences on mortality after myocardial infarction. *N Engl J Med* 1984;11:552–559.
10. Adler N, Boyce T, Chesney M, et al. Socioeconomic inequities in health: no easy solution. *JAMA* 1993;269:3140–3145.
11. Marmot MG, Kogeninas M, Elston MA. Social/economic status and disease. *Annu Rev Public Health* 1987;8:111–135.
12. Williams DR. Socioeconomic differentials in health: a review and redirection. *Soc Psychol Q* 1990;32:81–99.
13. Farley R, Allen W. *The color line and quality of life in America.* New York: Oxford University Press, 1987.
14. Jaynes G, Williams R Jr. *A common destiny: blacks and American society.* Washington, D.C.: National Academy Press, 1989.
15. Pappas G, Queen S, Hadden W, et al. The increasing disparity and mortality between socioeconomic groups in the United States, 1960 and 1986. *N Engl J Med* 1993;329:103–109.
16. Keil J, Tyroler H, Sandifer S. Hypertension: the effects of social class and racial admixture: the results of a cohort study in the black population of Charleston, South Carolina. *Am J Pub Health* 1977;67:634–639.
17. Wilson WJ. *The truly disadvantaged: the inner city, the underclass, and public policy.* Chicago: University of Chicago Press, 1987.
18. Haan MN, Kaplan GA, Camacho T. Poverty and health: prospective evidence from the Alameda County study. *Am J Epidemiol* 1987;125:989–998.
19. House J, Landis K, Umberson D. Social relationships and health. *Science* 1988;241:540–545.
20. Bullard RD. *Dumping in Dixie: race, class, and environmental quality.* Boulder, CO: Westview Press, 1994.
21. Kessler R, Neighbors H. A new perspective on the relationship among race, social class and psychological distress. *J Health Soc Behav* 1986;27:107–115.
22. Novotny T, Warner K, Kendrick J, et al. Smoking by blacks and whites: socioeconomic and demographic differences. *Am J Pub Health* 1988;78:1187–1189.
23. Kumanyika S. Obesity in black women. *Epidemiol Rev* 1987;9:31.
24. Gillum RF. Overweight and obesity in black women: a review of published data from the National Center for Health Statistics. *J Natl Med Assoc* 1987;79:865.
25. Blumenthal JA, Jiang W, Babyak MA, et al. Stress management and exercise training in cardiac patients with myocardial ischemia: effects on prognosis and evaluation of mechanisms. *Arch Intern Med* 1997;157:2213–2223.
26. NIH Technology Assessment Panel. The integration of behavioral relaxation approaches into the treatment of chronic pain and insomnia. *JAMA* 1996;226:313–318.
27. Fawzy FI, Fawzy NW, Hyun CS, et al. Malignant melanoma: effects of an early structured psychiatric intervention, coping, and affective state on recurrence and survival 6 years later. *Arch Gen Psychiatry* 1993;50:681–689.
28. Spiegel D, Bloom JR, Kraemer HC, Gottheil E. Effect of psychosocial treatment on survival of patients with metastatic breast cancer. *Lancet* 1989;2:888–890.

29. Alexander CN, Barnes VA, Schneider RH, et al. A randomized controlled trial of stress reduction on cardiovascular and all cause mortality: a 15 year follow-up on the effects of transcendental meditation, mindfulness and relaxation. *Circulation* 1996;93:629(abst).
30. Barnes V, Schneider R, Alexander C, Staggers F. Stress, stress reduction, and hypertension in African-Americans: an updated review. *J Nat Med Assoc* 1997;89:464–476.
31. Brown SA. Studies of educational interventions and outcomes in diabetic adults: a meta-analysis revisited. *Patient Educ Couns* 1990;16:189–215.
32. Delamater AM, Bubb J, Davis SG, et al. Randomized prospective study of self-management training with newly diagnosed diabetic children. *Diabetes Care* 1990;13:492–498.
33. Malone JM, Snyder M, Anderson G, Bernhard VM, Holloway GA Jr, Bunt TJ. Prevention of amputation by diabetic education. *Am J Surg* 1989;158:520–524.
34. Pallak MS, Cummings NA, Dorken H, Henke CJ. Effect of mental health treatment on medical costs. *Mind/Body Med* 1995;1:7–12.
35. Lorig K, Mazonson PD, Holman HR. Evidence suggesting that health education for self-management in patients with chronic arthritis has sustained health benefits while reducing health care costs. *Arthritis Rheum* 1993;36:439–446.
36. Caudill M, Schnable R, Zuttermeister P, Benson H, Friedman R. Decreased clinic use by chronic pain patients: response to behavioral medicine interventions. *Clin J Pain* 1991;7:305–310.
37. Robinson JS, Schwartz MM, Magwene KS, Krengel SA, Tamburello D. The impact of fever health education on clinic utilization. *Am J Dis Child* 1989;143:698–704.
38. Devine EC. Effects of psychoeducational care for adult surgical patients: a meta-analysis of 191 studies. *Patient Educ Couns* 1992;19:129–142.
39. Kennell J, Klaus M, McGrath S, Robertson S, Hinkley C. Continuous emotional support during labor in a U.S. hospital: a randomized controlled trial. *JAMA* 1991;265:2197–2237.
40. Klaus MK, Kennell J, Berkowitz G, Klaus P. Maternal assistance and support in labor: father, nurse, midwife, or doula? *Clin Consult Obstet Gynecol* 1992;4:211–217.
41. Prochaska J, DiClimente C. Stages and processes of self-change in smoking: toward an integrative model of change. *J Clin Psychol* 1983;51:390–395.

4

Substance Abuse: Health Care Implications

Louis L. Cregler

Academic Affairs and Department of Medicine, City University of New York Medical School, New York, New York 10031 and Department of Medicine, Maimonides Medical Center, Brooklyn, New York 11219

The use of cocaine, alcohol, steroids, heroin, amphetamines, marijuana, tobacco, and other agents is extremely prevalent in the United States and represents a significant public health problem (1–9). Cocaine-related medical events have escalated since the mid-1980s. In 1985, 30 million Americans used cocaine and 6 million were regular users (10). In 1996, the National Institute of Drug Abuse released data showing that 22 million Americans had used cocaine at least once in their lifetimes, and 4 million had used cocaine during the past year. This is a significant decrease in cocaine use from its peak in 1985 (3).

The use of drugs by high-profile entertainers and competitive athletes is common knowledge (Table 4-1). The prevalence of drug abuse is higher in urban areas, and minorities and women are especially vulnerable. Cocaine use among women is often connected with issues of sexuality and courtship (6–7,11). In 1994, 30.5 million of 98.4 million U.S. women had used an illicit drug at least once (6); at least 222,000 women had used an illicit drug during pregnancy in 1994 (3–4).

Cocaine use is not a new phenomenon. Coca leaves were chewed for their euphoric effects by the Indian population in South America as early as 600 A.D. (12–13). The soft drink Coca-Cola and many medications, cough syrups, tonics, and home remedies contained cocaine until 1914, when the Harrison Narcotic Act of 1914 prohibited the use of cocaine for nonmedicinal purposes.

PHARMACOLOGY AND PHARMACOKINETICS

Cardiopulmonary events are the most serious adverse effects seen in individuals seeking emergency care for cocaine abuse (14–18). The adverse cardiac consequences of cocaine can be appreciated best if the basic pharmacology of the drug is understood. Cocaine belongs to the class of agents known as *local anesthetics*, and comprises a benzene ring, an alcohol molecule, and a terminal amino side chain (19). Differences in potency, euphoric effect, and addictive properties depend on the terminal amino chain. Cocaine hydrochloride is heat labile and water soluble, melts at

TABLE 4-1. *Cocaine: special populations at risk*

Entertainers	Professionals
Actors	Bankers
Athletes	Engineers
Comedians	Health care providers
Musicians	Lawyers
Singers	Physicians

195°C, and is 89% cocaine by weight. Crack cocaine (alkaloid) is soluble in alcohol, acetone, ether, and oils but is insoluble in water. Crack is heat-stable, melts at 98°C, vaporizes, and can be smoked.

The rate of onset and duration of effects of cocaine depend on the route of administration. After smoking, the effects persist for 15 to 20 minutes and are comparable to those produced by intravenous administration. Intranasal cocaine provides effects lasting 1 to 2 hours. Cocaine is lipophilic, which accounts for its appearance in higher concentrations in the brain than in plasma. It blocks the reuptake of norepinephrine, often resulting in tachycardia, vasoconstriction, higher blood pressure, ventricular arrhythmias, and seizures. Its impairment of the reuptake of dopamine in the central nervous system is responsible for the sense of euphoria that occurs after use.

Cocaine is detoxified by the liver and plasma cholinesterase to water-soluble metabolites excreted in urine (20). Plasma cholinesterase activity is genetically determined and is lower in those with liver disease, during pregnancy, and in infants (21). Succinylcholine-sensitive individuals and people with congential cholinesterase deficiency have impaired detoxification of cocaine *in vivo*.

MYOCARDIAL INFARCTION

Reports of cocaine-related myocardial infarctions first appeared in the medical literature after cocaine use escalated in 1982 (22–33). Cardiac catheterization in patients younger than age 40 years reveals minimal angiographic evidence of coronary artery disease (22–24,27,28). Two-thirds of these events have been Q wave infarctions with a mortality rate of 10% (34). Cocaine produces vasoconstriction of normal coronary arteries, and the effect is enhanced at the site of atherosclerotic narrowing (35–36). The etiology of cocaine-induced myocardial infarction suggests focal coronary spasm or a thrombus or both (37–39). Myocardial infarction has been reported after small doses of cocaine, in first-time users, and with all routes of administration.

CEREBROVASCULAR ACCIDENT

A number of individuals have experienced cocaine-induced stroke during use (40–53). The mechanism is probably a sudden rise in arterial blood pressure due to adrenergic stimulation in a person with a berry aneurysm or an arteriovenous malformation (19). Subarachnoid hemorrhage, intracerebral hemorrhage, and ischemic stroke located in all vascular distributions have been described after cocaine use (54). Headache after cocaine use may be due to intracranial hemorrhage. Stroke occurs in patients with normal as well as diseased cerebral vessels, but individuals with abnormal cerebral vessels are at greater risk when using cocaine (50). Strokes have been reported in neonates and infants after cocaine exposure (55–58).

ARRHYTHMIAS

Arrhythmias occur during myocarditis, myocardial infarction, and cocaine intoxication (59–61). Impaired impulse conduction in the atrioventricular node and the His-Purkinje system occurs after cocaine use (62,63). Arrhythmias induced by cocaine include atrioventricular block, brady- and tachyarrhythmias, and asystole (64–68). Cocaine also has the potential to unmask accessory pathways, resulting in life-threatening cardiac arrhythmias. Sudden death after cocaine use has been reported in competitive athletes with no structural heart disease.

CARDIOMYOPATHY

Myocarditis is a common autopsy finding in cocaine abusers. One pathologist reported a 20% incidence of myocarditis in victims dying of cocaine abuse, as opposed to 3.7% in controls (69). The foci of myocarditis are composed of lymphocytes and eosinophils, which may suggest that the origin of cocaine-induced myocarditis is a hypersensitivity reaction. Dilated cardiomyopathy has been attributed to cocaine abuse (70–75). Cocaine abuse may lead to interstitial fibrosis and congestive heart failure.

GREATER RISK FOR WOMEN

More than 9 million women of all ages, races, and cultures used illegal drugs during 1997. Of these, 2 million were cocaine users. Seventy percent of all acquired immunodeficiency syndrome cases among women are drug-related (7). Cocaine use during pregnancy has a deleterious effect on the mother and fetus (Table 4-2) (8,76); almost all drugs cross the placenta and enter the bloodstream of the fetus. Ruptured aortic

TABLE 4-2. *Risks in pregnant women using cocaine*

Unborn child	Mother
Prematurity	Spontaneous abortion
Low birth weight	Abruptio placentae
Stillbirth	Ectopic pregnancy
Strokes	Toxicity
Sudden infant death syndrome	Sexually transmitted diseases and human immunodeficiency virus/acquired immunodeficiency syndrome
Congenital anomalies	Nutritional deficiencies
? IQ issues	Death

TABLE 4-3. *Characteristics of women who abuse drugs*

70% were sexually abused
80% had an addicted parent
Low self-esteem
Little self-confidence
Lonely and depressed
Physically abused
Isolated from positive support networks
Initiated into drug use by male sex partners

aneurysms, pulmonary edema, infectious endocarditis, and vascular thrombosis occur in cocaine abusers. Cocaine-related events in the pregnant woman and fetus include an increased incidence of spontaneous abortion, abruptio placentae, and congenital anomalies of the fetus (77). Cardiac malformations include ventricular and atrial septal defect, transposition of the great vessels, and hypoplastic right heart syndrome.

Seventy percent of women who use drugs were sexually abused before age 16 years and 80% had at least one parent who was addicted to alcohol or drugs. These women often have low self-esteem, lack confidence, are isolated from support networks, and feel powerless (Table 4-3). Most women report that they are initiated into drug abuse by a male sex partner who also hinders their efforts to seek treatment. Often, women do not seek treatment because they fear the loss of their children, punishment by law enforcement agencies, or reprisal by a boyfriend or spouse (3).

MANAGEMENT

The evaluation of any cocaine abuser with chest pain is challenging. Chest pain must be presumed to be ischemic in origin until proven otherwise (78). Electrocardiograms should be done on patients with chest pain, and must be read with caution because persistent juvenile ST segment repolarization changes may also represent myocardial ischemia. Patients with unexplained cardiovascular symptoms should be asked about cocaine use, and a drug screen should be ordered when indicated.

Propranolol may be given in cocaine intoxication but can result in paradoxic hypertension. Labetalol is given intravenously to control severe hypertension associated with cocaine use. Beta blockers are recommended for their effects on the hyperadrenergic state and supraventricular and ventricular arrhythmias. In acute myocardial infarction, the use of a short-acting agent, such as esmolol, is indicated (64). Nitrates and calcium channel and alpha-adrenergic blockers are useful in the treatment of cocaine-related ischemia.

CONCLUSIONS

Changing patterns of cocaine use have led to an increased incidence of cocaine-related cardiovascular complications. Cocaine use can be fatal, and cardiac complications and death occur in first-time users regardless of route or dosage. Preexisting heart disease is not a prerequisite for experiencing a cocaine-related cardiac event. Myocardial infarction in any patient who displays no cardiovascular risk factors should alert the physician to the possibility of cocaine abuse. Women are at greater risk for adverse cardiac and health consequences because of lower cholinesterase levels. In addition, cocaine use during pregnancy has a deleterious effect on both mother and fetus. Physicians encountering unexplained cardiovascular events, including malignant hypertension, stroke, cardiomyopathy, congestive heart failure, and other vascular events, should ask about cocaine abuse.

REFERENCES

1. National Institute on Drug Abuse. *NIDA capsules: anabolic steroid abuse.* Available at http://www.nida.nih.gov/NIDACapsules/NCSteroids.html.
2. National Institute on Drug Abuse. *NIDA capsules: methamphetamines abuse.* Available at http://www.nida.nih.gov/NIDACapsules/NCMethamphetamine.html.
3. National Institute on Drug Abuse. *NIDA capsules: cocaine abuse.* Available at http://www.nida.nih.gov/NIDACapsules/NCCocaine.html.
4. National Institute on Drug Abuse. *NIDA capsules: cigarette smoking.* Available at http://www.nida.nih.gov/NIDACapsules/NCCigs.html.
5. National Institute on Drug Abuse. *NIDA capsules: marijuana update.* Available at http://www.nida.nih.gov/NIDACapsules/NCMarijuana.html.
6. National Institute on Drug Abuse. *NIDA capsules: women and drug abuse.* Available at http://www.nida.nih.gov/NIDACapsules/NCWomen.html.
7. National Institute on Drug Abuse. *Women and drug abuse.* Available at http://www.nida.nih.gov/WomenDrugs/Women-DrugAbuse.html.
8. National Institute on Drug Abuse. *Drug use during pregnancy.* Available at http://165.112.78.61/NIDA_Notes/NNVol10N1/Pregnancytable.html.
9. National Institute on Drug Abuse. *NIDA capsules: designer drugs.* Available at http://www.nida.nih.gov/NIDACapsules/NCDesigner.html.
10. Abelson HI, Miller JD. A decade of trends in cocaine use in the household population. *NIDA Res Monogr* 1985;61:35–49.
11. Washton AM. Women and cocaine. *Med Aspects Hum Sex* 1986;20(3):57.
12. Freud S. On coca. In: Byck R, ed. *Cocaine papers.* New York: Stonehill Publishing Co., 1974:49–73.
13. Siegel RK. Cocaine smoking. *J Psychoactive Drugs* 1982;13:271–343.
14. Lowenstein DH, Massa SM, Rowbotham MC, Collins SD, McKinney HE, Simon RP. Acute neurologic and psychiatric complications associated with cocaine abuse. *Am J Med* 1987;83(1):841–846.
15. Cregler LL. Acute neurologic and psychiatric complications associated with cocaine abuse [Letter]. *Am J Med* 1988;84(5):978–979.
16. Brody SL, Slovis CM, Wrenn KD. Cocaine-related medical problems: consecutive series of 233 patients. *Am J Med* 1990;88(5):325–331.
17. Billman GE. Mechanisms responsible for the cardiotoxic effects of cocaine. *FASEB J* 1990;4:2469–2475.
18. Gawin FH, Ellinwood EH Jr. Cocaine and other stimulants. *N Engl J Med* 1988;318(18):1173–1182.
19. Cregler LL, Mark H. Medical complications of cocaine abuse. *N Engl J Med* 1986;315(23):1495–1500.
20. Stewart DJ, Inaba T, Lucassen M, et al. Cocaine metabolism: cocaine and norcocaine hydrolysis by liver and serum esterases. *Clin Pharmacol Ther* 1979;25:464–468.
21. Om A, Ellahham S, Ornato JP, et al. Medical complications of cocaine: possible relationship to low plasma cholinesterase enzyme. *Am Heart J* 1993;125(4):1114–1117.
22. Cregler LL, Mark H. Relation of acute myocardial infarction to cocaine abuse. *Am J Cardiol* 1985;56:794.
23. Kossowsky WA, Lyon AF. Cocaine and acute myocardial infarction: a probable connection. *Chest* 1984;85:729–731.
24. Howard RE, Hueter DC, Davis GJ. Acute myocardial infarction following cocaine abuse in a young woman with normal coronary arteries. *JAMA* 1985;254:95–96.

25. Weiss RJ. Recurrent myocardial infarction caused by cocaine abuse. *Am Heart J* 1986;111:793.
26. Simpson RW, Edwards WD. Pathogenesis of cocaine-induced ischemic heart disease. *Arch Pathol Lab Med* 1986;110:479–484.
27. Isner JM, Estes NAM III, Thompson PD, et al. Acute cardiac events temporally related to cocaine abuse. *N Engl J Med* 1986;315:1438–1443.
28. Myers GH, Hansen TH, Jain A. Left main coronary artery and femoral artery vasospasm associated with cocaine use. *Chest* 1991;100(1):257–258.
29. Rollinger IM, Belzberg AS, MacDonald IL. Cocaine-induced myocardial infarction. *CMAJ* 1986;135:45–46.
30. Rod JL, Zucker RP. Acute myocardial infarction shortly after cocaine inhalation. *Am J Cardiol* 1987;59:161.
31. Zimmerman FH, Gustafson GM, Kemp HG. Recurrent myocardial infarction associated with cocaine abuse in a young man with normal coronary arteries: evidence for coronary artery spasm culminating in thrombosis. *J Am Coll Cardiol* 1987;9(4):964–968.
32. Smith HWB, Liberman HA, Brody SL, Battey LL, Donahue BC, Morris DC. Acute myocardial infarction temporally related to cocaine use. *Ann Intern Med* 1987;107:13–18.
33. Kossowsky WA, Lyon AF, Chou SY. Acute non-Q wave cocaine-related myocardial infarction. *Chest* 1989;96(3):617–621.
34. Lange RA, Flores ED, Cigarroa RG, Hillis LD. Cocaine-induced myocardial ischemia and infarction. *Cardiology* 1990;74–79.
35. Flores ED, Lange RA, Cigarroa RG, Hillis LD. Effect of cocaine on coronary artery dimensions in atherosclerotic coronary artery disease: enhanced vasoconstriction at sites of significant stenoses. *J Am Coll Cardiol* 1990;16:74–79.
36. Chokshi SK, Miller G, Rongione A, Isner JM. Cocaine and cardiovascular diseases: the leading edge. *Cardiology* 1989;76[Suppl 3]:1–6.
37. Vincent GM, Anderson JL, Marshall HW. Coronary spasm producing coronary thrombosis and myocardial infarction. *N Engl J Med* 1983;309:220–223.
38. Stenberg RG, Winniford MD, Hillis LD, Dowling GP, Buja LM. Simultaneous acute thrombosis of two major coronary arteries following intravenous cocaine use. *Arch Pathol Lab Med* 1989;113(5):521–524.
39. Fernandez MS, Pichard AD, Marchant E, Lindsay J Jr. Acute myocardial infarction with normal coronary arteries: in vivo demonstration of coronary thrombosis during the acute episode. *Clin Cardiol* 1983;6:553–559.
40. Petty GW, Brust JC, Tatemichi TK, Barr ML. Embolic stroke after smoking "crack" cocaine. *Stroke* 1990;21(11):1632–1635.
41. Lichtenfeld PJ, Rubin DB, Feldman RS. Subarachnoid hemorrhage precipitated by cocaine snorting. *Arch Neurol* 1984;41:223–224.
42. Caplan LR, Hier DB, Banks G. Current concepts of cerebrovascular disease–stroke: stroke and drug abuse. *Stroke* 1982;13:869–872.
43. Golbe LI, Merkin MD. Cerebral infarction in a user of free-base cocaine ("crack"). *Neurology* 1986;36:1602–1604.
44. Wojak JC, Flamm ES. Intracranial hemorrhage and cocaine use. *Stroke* 1987;18(4):712–715.
45. Tuchman AJ, Daras M, Zalzal P, Mangiardi J. Intracranial hemorrhage after cocaine abuse. *JAMA* 1987;257(9):1175.
46. Levine SR, Welch KMA. Cocaine and stroke. *Stroke* 1988;19(6):779–783.
47. Seaman ME. Acute cocaine abuse associated with cerebral infarction. *Ann Emerg Med* 1990;19(1):34–37.
48. Nolte KB, Gelman BB. Intracerebral hemorrhage associated with cocaine abuse. *Arch Pathol Lab Med* 1989;113(7):812–813.
49. Mangiardi JR, Daras M, Geller ME, Weitzer I, Tuchman AJ. Cocaine-related intracranial hemorrhage. *Acta Neurol Scand* 1988;77(3):177–180.
50. Cregler LL, Mark H. Relation of stroke to cocaine abuse. *N Y State J Med* 1987;87:129–130.
51. Kaye BR, Fainstat M. Cerebral vasculitis associated with cocaine abuse. *JAMA* 1987;258:2104–2106.
52. Henderson CE, Torbey M. Rupture of intracranial aneurysm associated with cocaine abuse during pregnancy. *Am J Perinatol* 1988;5:142–143.
53. Mercado A, Johnson G Jr, Calver D, Sokol RJ. Cocaine, pregnancy and postpartum intracerebral hemorrhage. *Obstet Gynecol* 1989;73:467–468.
54. Rowbotham MC. Neurologic aspects of cocaine abuse. *West J Med* 1988;149:442–448.

55. Chasnoff IJ, Bussey ME, Savich R, Stack CM. Perinatal cerebral infarction and maternal cocaine use. *J Pediatr* 1986;108:456–459.
56. Spires MC, Gordon EF, Choudhuri M, Maldonado E, Chan R. Intracranial hemorrhage in a neonate following prenatal cocaine exposure. *Pediatr Neurol* 1989;5(5):324–326.
57. Oro AS, Dixon SD. Perinatal cocaine and methamphetamine exposure: maternal and neonatal correlates. *J Pediatr* 1987;111:571–578.
58. Chasnoff IJ, Griffith DR, MacGregor S, Dirkes K, Burns KA. Temporal patterns of cocaine use in pregnancy, perinatal outcome. *JAMA* 1989;261:1741–1744.
59. Vignola PA, Aonuma K, Swaye PS, et al. Lymphocytic myocarditis presenting as unexplained ventricular arrhythmias: diagnosis with endomyocardial biopsy and response to immunosuppression. *J Am Coll Cardiol* 1984;4(4):812–819.
60. Jonsson S, O'Meara M, Young J. Acute cocaine poisoning: importance of treating seizures and acidosis. *Am J Med* 1983;75:1061–1064.
61. Gradman AH. Cardiac effects of cocaine: a review. *Yale J Biol Med* 1988;61:137–147.
62. Blumenthal RS, Flaherty JT. Recognizing cardiac crisis in cocaine abusers. *J Crit Illness* 1990;5(3): 225–239.
63. Cregler LL, Swartz MH, Go A, Lee L, Mark H. The effects of cocaine on the electrocardiogram. *Alcohol Clin Exp Res* 1988;12(1):191.
64. Nanji AA, Filipenko JD. Asystole and ventricular fibrillation associated with cocaine intoxication. *Chest* 1984;85:132–133.
65. Benchimol A, Bartall H, Desser KB. Accelerated ventricular rhythm and cocaine abuse. *Ann Intern Med* 1978;88:519–520.
66. Billman GE, Hoskins RS. Cocaine-induced ventricular fibrillation: protection afforded by the calcium antagonist verapamil. *FASEB J* 1988;2(14):2990–2995.
67. Om A, Ellenbogen KA, Vetrovec GW. Cocaine-induced bradyarrhythmias. *Am Heart J* 1992;124(1):232–233.
68. Geggel RL, McInerny J, Estes NAM III. Transient neonatal ventricular tachycardia associated with maternal cocaine use. *Am J Cardiol* 1989;63:383–384.
69. Virmani R, Robinowitz M, Smialek JE, Symth DF. Cardiovascular effects of cocaine: an autopsy study of 40 patients. *Am J Med* 1988;115(5):1068–1076.
70. Duell PB. Chronic cocaine abuse and dilated cardiomyopathy [Letter]. *Am J Med* 1987;83:601.
71. Hoffman CK, Goodman PC. Pulmonary edema in cocaine smokers. *Radiology* 1989;172:463–465.
72. Weiner RS, Lockhart JT, Schwart RG. Dilated cardiomyopathy and cocaine abuse: report of two cases. *Am J Med* 1986;81:699–701.
73. Chokshi SK, Moore R, Pandian NG, Isner JM. Reversible cardiomyopathy associated with cocaine intoxication. *Ann Intern Med* 1989;11(12):1039–1040.
74. Peng SK, French WJ, Pelikan PC. Direct cocaine cardiotoxicity demonstrated by endomyocardial biopsy. *Arch Pathol Lab Med* 1989;113(8):842–845.
75. Bertolet BD, Freund G, Martin CA, Perchalski DL, Williams CM, Pepine CJ. Unrecognized left ventricular dysfunction in an apparently healthy cocaine abuse population. *Clin Cardiol* 1990;13(5):323–328.
76. Mayock DE, Ramey SL, Moore L. Cocaine and the use of alcohol and other drugs during pregnancy. *Am J Obstet Gynecol* 1991;164:1239–1243.
77. Perper JA, Van Thiel DH. Cardiovascular complications of cocaine abuse. *Recent Dev Alcohol* 1992;10:343–361.
78. Goldfrank L. Consultations. *Ann Emerg Med* 1987;16:240.

5

Role of Medical Ethics in the Training of Physicians

Marian Gray Secundy

Department of Community Health and Family Practice, Program in Clinical Ethics, Howard University College of Medicine, Washington, D.C. 20059

Advances in science and technology increasingly stimulate concern about the associated ethical issues. The practice of medicine has become more and more complex, as have the choices that patients and their doctors must make. Historically, physicians have acknowledged duties and obligations to their patients. Those duties and obligations have been rooted in an ethical tradition grounded in principles of beneficence, fidelity, and justice for the physician and autonomy for the patient.

The physician's mandate has always been to do no harm, tell the truth, respect the patient, and maintain patient confidentiality. The medical codes of ethics of early historical periods all speak in some way to these duties and obligations (Hippocratic Oath, Oath of Maimonides, and so forth). The medical profession has also had unwritten expectations of itself that accompanied those duties and obligations. These commitments to professional etiquette and courtesy have been self-protective and self-serving in many instances, but at the same time they have preserved and maintained a certain order. The duties and obligations have been implicit throughout the history of the profession. Rarely were they explicitly addressed or critically analyzed; the lessons were taught by example and learned at the bedside (1).

In the mid-1970s, however, theologians and philosophers began to ask hard questions about the medical enterprise and about medical decision making and the effects of modern scientific advances on patient care. Physicians themselves began to wonder about the moral issues that were surfacing as technological advances became more available. Paul Ramsey (2,3) and Joseph Fletcher (4,5), among others, began to ask questions about the nature of personhood and the dignity of human life. The ability to extend life, to maintain some form of life by artificial means, and to transplant organs prompted a focused look at the meaning of the medical profession's commitment to do no harm, to be beneficent, and to be just. Definitions of death were reexamined and expanded. The cessation of vital life signs was augmented, some would say supplanted, as the defining moment of death by the Harvard criteria for brain death (6). Patients began to engage actively in debates about life and its maintenance by extra-

TABLE 5-1. *Goals of medicine*

Promotion of health and prevention of disease
Relief of symptoms, pain, and suffering
Cure of disease
Preventing untimely death
Improvement of functional status or maintenance of compromised status
Education and counseling of patients regarding their condition and prognosis
Avoiding harm to the patient in the course of care

ordinary means. Traditional and heretofore acceptable paternalism in physicians began to be challenged by those who wanted to participate more actively in decisions about their own lives and the lives of their loved ones. Health care costs began to escalate, and the high costs associated with dying were challenged by policy makers, insurance companies, and consumers. Questions about the appropriate limits of medicine, about the responsibility of balancing patient values with the medical goal of maintaining life at all costs, and about the medical professional's obligation to allow patients more autonomy were asked more and more frequently (Table 5-1). Simultaneously, an acknowledgment of past violations related to research on human subjects generated the Belmont Report (subtitled "ethical principles and guidelines for the protection of human subjects of research") (7) and federal regulations protective of future subjects of scientific inquiry. Attention to matters of informed consent in nontherapeutic as well as therapeutic settings became a central focus of medical ethics literature.

Medical education slowly began to take a look at itself. It became apparent that practicing physicians had not been adequately prepared to deal with these questions on either a personal or professional basis. Several medical sociologists observed that much of physicians' inadequacy appeared to stem from the lack of appropriate mechanisms for managing issues related to uncertainty, death, dying, and communication with patients about decision making in these and other sensitive areas (8–13) (Table 5-2). The curriculum gradually changed with the introduction of courses that addressed both cognitive and affective aspects of patient management and patient self-awareness. These courses focused on many of the ethical issues inherent in reconciling the dilemmas posed by integrating technology and its promises with patient wishes. Today, few would challenge the value of courses in medical and clinical ethics that help physicians develop more effective analytical and problem-solving skills to use when confronted with value conflicts in patient care.

The scope of inquiry and interest has expanded beyond end-of-life decisions. Although discussion of end-of-life quandaries constitutes much of the prolific liter-

TABLE 5-2. *Decision-making considerations*

Medical indications
Patient preferences
External factors
Quality-of-life issues

ature on medical ethics, more and more physicians and other health professionals are addressing ethical problems raised by other aspects of scientific inquiry. For example, advances in reproductive and genetic technologies, the management of new communicable diseases, such as acquired immunodeficiency syndrome (AIDS), and the implications of increased attention to issues of health care costs pose numerous dilemmas for physicians and patients. Matters of scientific integrity and the protection of human subjects in research settings are ever-present. Practicing physicians and other health professionals must deal with ethical dilemmas raised at both micro (patient care) and macro (societal) levels.

Responses are found in medical education at a variety of levels and from a variety of approaches. For the most part, medical students are taught through elective offerings, lectures within required courses (e.g., "Introduction to Patient Care"), and, in most schools, required or elective courses in medical ethics. Residents receive an occasional grand rounds presentation, and in some very advanced situations participate in a specified series of required lectures and discussions. Occasionally ethics faculty or consultants accompany residents and students in various clinical settings on patient rounds. Ethics committees or consultation services exist in a good number of hospitals and present other opportunities for dialogue between and education of attending physicians. The Joint Commission of American Health Care Organizations accreditation criteria require specific attention to matters of medical and organizational ethics. There are a plethora of conferences for the practicing physician that offer continuing medical education credits and address a myriad of ethical problems in medicine and in health care in general. Only rarely do ethnic Americans or people of color take advantage of these opportunities, however, perhaps because the offerings appear to lack specific relevance.

An issue of continuing concern is the relative lack of attention to the ethical issues that are most important to communities of color in the United States. Intellectual arguments about medical ethics have been defined and framed from a distinctly Eurocentric perspective by a select group of analytical philosophers and theologians with very little awareness of the complexities presented by various culturally diverse perspectives. The number of formally trained bioethicists of color is very small, as is the number of spokespersons of color with related expertise or interests. The role of individual autonomy in decision making; how to communicate appropriately with persons of various socioeconomic and cultural backgrounds; and the effects of a cost-containment focus on the disempowered, the disadvantaged, and the underserved are specific ethical dilemmas needing greater attention. The historically relevant problems associated with the inclusion and exclusion of people of color in research on human subjects presents a particularly difficult problem. The topics addressed in mainstream conferences on medical ethics are rarely framed with any reference to other voices that must be identified and heard. The advent of the feminist movement in bioethics heralds some positive change in this pattern. The work of the Program in Clinical Ethics at Howard University, Washington, D.C.; the newly formed Center for Bioethics and Health Care Research at Tuskegee Institute, Tuskegee, Alabama; and the potential represented by the Minority Health Institute in Los Angeles hold great promise for increasing the number of minority voices in medical ethics that address those issues of greatest relevance to the minority community.

Howard University has offered a required course in medical ethics since the 1970s. The 1990s have seen an exciting innovation: A required course has been created not only for medical students but for students from all of Howard's five schools and colleges in the health sciences. Students of medicine, allied health, nursing, pharmacy, and dentistry come together in lectures and small group sessions to discuss the traditional ethical issues facing their professions and to weigh the significance that those issues hold for them as primary health care providers of color serving a patient population predominantly of color. Howard University is perhaps the most internationally diverse university in America, and every year 20 to 50 different countries are represented in the student population of the Health Care Ethics course. More than one-third of the students speak English as a second language. Observations from questionnaires taken over a 4-year period indicate high concern with issues of health care reform, AIDS, and end-of-life care. Student discussions reflect deep suspicion and distrust of genetic technologies. Further in-depth research documenting the reasons for this distrust is needed. Anecdotal evidence and limited research (14,15) suggest that African-American physicians in particular are less likely to opt for limitations in care when providing advanced directive information than are white American doctors. More research is needed here as well. However, a cursory assessment of Howard University's faculty's and students' opinions on the matter of physician-assisted suicide, especially as it relates to racial matters, does not show differences from mainstream reports. Clearly, there are indications that health professionals could work more effectively with patients of diverse backgrounds.

There are numerous issues to be raised with all health care professionals in training and in practice. Often, teachers of ethics are challenged by those who wonder if one can in fact teach morality or ethics. The objective is not, however, to teach morality or ethics per se, but rather to encourage rational and thoughtful reflection on ethical problems in patient care and ethical issues in the delivery of health care. Critical analysis and critical approaches to problem solving and the development of public policy are desirable ends of any cognitive or affective strategy for instruction in ethics. Less clear are the proper timing for the introduction of various ethical dilemmas and the ideal methods for focusing the attention of health care providers, in particular clinicians, on key ethical questions. Providers who are able to recognize an ethical problem and distinguish it from a legal question or a failure of communication with the patient are well situated to impact on the ethical problems of their patients. The next stage, developing the capacity for logically finding workable decision-making strategies that involve, when possible, the patient, his or her family, and the health care team, is necessary and is probably an ongoing, never-ending process. The extent to which individual providers ought (in the moral sense) to become involved in issues of advocacy regarding public policy in health care is quite controversial. There are those who believe that patient care for minority populations requires advocacy from those who deliver it as an essential prerequisite for dealing with the realities of a minority population's health status. Advocacy may or may not be an "ought," but

TABLE 5-3. *Ethical dilemmas and tensions*

Limited resources and social justice
Determinations and criteria related to medical futility
Limitations on scientific inquiry
Public safety vs. individual rights

clearly awareness of all aspects of the problems engendered by the delivery of health care to various socioeconomic groups in our society is necessary. Health care providers are called on consciously to incorporate the influences of society as a whole on health status, health behavior, and institutional responses into their analyses of micro and macro ethical issues.

Appropriate ways to provide continuing education for practicing physicians in relevant areas of medical ethics are important areas for exploration. Seminars, workshops, and intensive training for health care providers of color, with particular emphasis on the significance of ethical issues to matters of race and class, are recommended. Clinicians and scientific investigators are needed to further the areas of inquiry and to serve on various scientific review groups and research teams so that objectivity and accuracy in all aspects of medical ethics are assured. Focus on the historical context in which ethical problems have surfaced is also necessary in the development of curriculum materials. For example, in addition to raising and addressing questions about micro and macro issues related to abortion, euthanasia, physician-assisted suicide, genetic technologies, organ transplantation, and so forth, attention must be given to the meaning of past and current violations of the rights of human research subjects and of patients receiving care. Several of the issues that might be examined in various continuing education programs are listed in Table 5-3. Case materials, experiential exercises, literature, and drama, as well as traditional written materials from books and journals, are effective in stimulating dialogue and interest. There should be clarity about the goals of continuing education activities and most especially an awareness that medical ethics does not provide easy solutions or recipes but tools of analysis and models of decision making. Medical ethics does not minimize uncertainty; in fact, uncertainty is often heightened as providers confront the reality of tragic decisions that must be made in many instances. Nevertheless, it is desirable to eliminate irrational responses and to be fully aware of the meaning of actions to self and others.

REFERENCES

1. Bean WB, ed. *Sir William Osler. Aphorisms from his bedside teachings and writings.* Springfield, IL: Charles C. Thomas, 1961.
2. Ramsey P. *Ethics at the edge of life: medical and legal intersections.* New Haven, CT: Yale University Press, 1980.
3. Ramsey P. *The patient as a person.* New Haven, CT: Yale University Press, 1984.
4. Fletcher J. *Humanhood: essays in biomedical ethics.* Buffalo, NY: Prometheus, 1979.

5. Fletcher J, Childress J. *Situation ethics: the new morality.* Louisville, KY: Westminster John Knox Press, 1966.
6. Report of the Ad Hoc Committee of the Harvard Medical School to Examine the Definition of Brain Death. A definition of irreversible coma. *JAMA* 1968;205:377–340.
7. National Commission for the Protection of Human Subjects of Biomedical and Behavioral Research. *The Belmont Report: ethical principles and guidelines for the protection of human subjects of research.* Washington: US Department of Health, Education, and Welfare, 1978.
8. Balint M. *Doctor, his patient and the illness.* Rome: International University Press, 1990.
9. Fox RC. *Essays in medical sociology: journeys into the field.* New Brunswick, NJ: Transaction Publishers, 1988.
10. Fox RC. *Experiment perilous: physicians and patients facing the unknown.* Philadelphia: University of Pennsylvania Press, 1974.
11. Fox RC. *The sociology of medicine: a participant observer's view.* Upper Saddle River, NJ: Prentice Hall, 1988.
12. Katz J. *The silent world of doctor and patient.* Baltimore: Johns Hopkins University Press, 1997.
13. Bosk CL. *Forgive and remember: managing medical fairness.* Chicago: University of Chicago, 1981.
14. Teno JM. Do formal advance directives affect resuscitation decisions and the use of resources for seriously ill patients? *J Clin Ethics* 1994;5(1):23–30.
15. Teno J, Lynn J, Connors AF Jr, et al. The illusion of end-of-life resources savings with advance directives. SUPPORT investigators. Study to understand prognoses and preferences for outcomes and risks of treatment. *J Am Geriatr Soc* 1997;45:513–518.

6

Medical and Legal Issues

B. Waine Kong, *Stephanie Kong, and †Jillian Kong-Sivert

*Association of Black Cardiologists, Inc., Atlanta, Georgia 30310; *Metrohealth, Atlanta, Georgia 30327; and †Office of Senator Barbara Mikulski, Washington, D.C. 20002*

As recently as the 1970s, physicians enjoyed what was arguably the highest level of trust and social approbation of all professionals. The old joke tells of a proud mother yelling, "Help, Help! My son, the doctor, is drowning!" At one time, physicians were above reproach. Who would have questioned the decisions of Drs. Marcus Welby and Ben Casey? Who would suggest prosecuting them for crimes against the state or suing them for malpractice?

There appears to be a shift in public perception. Physicians have been supplanted in many of their traditional roles, by pharmacists and technicians on the one hand and religious and spiritual leaders on the other, to such a degree that the public is more inclined to trust these professionals than physicians in medical matters (1). Furthermore, there is a trend throughout society against rigid social conventions that mask human fallibility, particularly those conventions that allow authority to stand unquestioned. One side effect of this breakdown in formality, which brings with it a welcome inducement to patients to increase their input and involvement, is that physicians are perceived to be "only human" and medicine "just a business." Physicians are losing the protection that social conventions once afforded. Ironically, the more humbly physicians behave, the more vulnerable they are to being characterized as mercenary.

In the 1990s, political rhetoric about health care, and health care finance in particular, has both contributed to and exploited this derogation of doctors. It is politically expedient for lawmakers that the public believes health care to be full of chicanery, and fraud to be the sole or principal factor in spiraling health care costs. According to Ken Abromowitz, a health industry analyst at Sanford Bernstein,

> Eighty percent of this new fraud push is politics. Medicare is five years from bankruptcy. They'd like people to believe it's because of greedy hospitals and doctors, not government incompetence and mismanagement (*USA Today*, August 6, 1997).

In a radio address to the nation on January 24, 1998, President Clinton said, "Medicare fraud is a real crime committed by real criminals intent on stealing from the system and cheating our most vulnerable citizens." He promised to save $2 billion each year by doubling audits of cost-based providers, allowing competitive bidding for equipment and nonphysician services, creating civil penalties for physicians who inappropriately certify patients for hospitalization, granting Medicare the right of first recovery when a provider files for bankruptcy, and banning Medicare providers from inflating prices on prescription drugs. A survey of the American Association of Retired Persons (AARP) shows that this was a promise likely to strike a chord in voters: Seventy percent of AARP members believe that the problem with Medicare financing is caused by fraud and abuse among health care providers (Anders G, McGinley L. A new kind of crime now stirs the feds: health care fraud. *The Wall Street Journal*, May 6, 1997).

Government agencies are calling for stricter and more complex laws in the field of health care and more rigorous and expansive enforcement of existing laws, with an eye toward generating revenue. As Kathryn Serkes of the Association of American Physicians and Surgeons explained of property confiscation under the Racketeer Influenced and Corrupt Organization chapter of the Organized Crime Control Act of 1970, "The government is now casting its ever expanding net . . . to ensnare the newest class of federally defined criminals: *doctors*. [The Health Care Financing Administration] is perpetuating a set of byzantine rules—virtually indecipherable for even the most scrupulous doctor" (Serkes K. Anti-gangster laws used against doctors. *The Wall Street Journal*, January 20, 1998). The complexity of these rules ensures a steady stream of civil and criminal fines.

The Health Care Portability and Accountability Act of 1996 authorized the Health Care Financing Administration (HCFA) to freeze physicians' assets on the mere suspicion of an intention to commit fraud. The U.S. Justice Department reported in 1997 that, as a result of a 60% increase in the number of civil health care cases initiated, $1 billion was recovered from 363 convictions (Clinton outlines rules to check Medicare fraud. *The Wall Street Journal*, January 26, 1998). If this trend continues, it is conceivable, given the triple-damages rule, that the government will eventually make a profit from government-sponsored health care entitlement programs.

From 1992 to 1996, Federal Bureau of Investigation (FBI) health care fraud investigations jumped from 657 to 2,200; in 1997 the number rose above 6,000. The government believes it still has a long way to go to clean up the system. According to a report issued by HCFA, $23 billion was wasted on fraudulent claims: 37% of that total for lack of medical necessity, 33% for insufficient documentation, 14% for lack of documentation, 9% for incorrect coding, 5% for noncovered or unallowable services, and 2% listed as other.

According to U.S. Secretary of Health and Human Services (HHS) Donna Shalala, fraud among physicians is endemic (2). The daily headlines are now familiar: "Federal authorities in Miami have charged a dozen people, including five doctors, with bilking the government out of $15 million in Medicare payments through a scheme that prosecutors portrayed as one of the nation's largest cases of home health fraud" (*The News Journal*, August 8, 1997). "With the nation's health system shuddering under the stress of massive changes, federal authorities have more than tripled their prosecutions and convictions for health care fraud since 1992" (*The Atlanta Journal/The Atlanta Constitution*, August 14, 1997). As health care payments by the government rise, fraud seizures soar. Medicare/Medicaid recoveries increased fourfold in just 1 year (Health Care Financing Administration, Department of Human Resources. *USA Today*, August 6, 1997).

Shalala has said, "Whenever I travel to a town-hall meeting, what people really want to talk about is health care waste, fraud and abuse" (Anders G, McGinley L. A new kind of crime now stirs the feds: health care fraud. *The Wall Street Journal*, May 6, 1997). As a result, HHS hired 200 new auditors to do nothing but investigate health care fraud, and every federal prosecutor's office now has a health care fraud coordinator. At the Internal Revenue Service, 150 employees in the 3,200-person criminal division now concentrate on health care fraud cases—nearly double the 80 employees that were thus occupied in 1995—and the Justice Department plans to hire more than 100 additional prosecutors specializing in health care fraud. The Kennedy/Kassebaum law created a $4-billion superfund to fight health care fraud. "Operation Restore Trust" is recovering $100 million each year.

Although the health care system was easy to defraud in the past, the FBI has revealed that agents and computer resources freed up by the end of the Cold War have been reassigned to investigating and prosecuting doctors (3). In a direct threat to doctors, Attorney General Janet Reno said, "We have the know-how, we have the resources, and we have the will to come after you" (*The Atlanta Journal/The Atlanta Constitution*, August 14, 1997). If this strikes terror in the hearts of physicians, that is the result the government is seeking. They hope to scare doctors into compliance with health care regulations.

Health care has become a highly regulated industry and a trap for physicians who "just want to practice medicine." It would not be an overstatement to say that doctors are under siege. According to Dr. Richard Davidson, President of the American Hospital Association, "The government's attitude now appears to be that we are guilty until proven innocent" (*USA Today*, August 6, 1997). He notes that, although honest mistakes, confusion over confusing rules, and disagreements over what patients need do occur, now everything is viewed as fraud and all doctors are under suspicion. Dr. Malcolm Sparrow, a lecturer on fraud at the Kennedy School of Government, agrees. In his book *License to Steal* he observes that, although some health care fraud is easy to identify, often the distinctions between fraud and upcoding, overbilling, and well-intentioned overtreatment are blurry (Anders G, McGinley L. A new kind of crime now stirs the feds: health care fraud. *The Wall Street Journal*, May 6, 1997). These efforts by the government obviously create a chilling environment for honest physicians.

FALSE CLAIMS ACT

Although the False Claims Act was not written with physicians in mind, this catch-all regulation has become the one most commonly invoked against physicians. The commonsense definition of a false claim requires that the physician present the claim to the government knowing that it is false, fictitious, or fraudulent. However, the requirement that the physician be aware of his or her wrongdoing and that this awareness be proved has been relaxed.

The effects of this laxity can be seen in the case of Dr. Clyde Brown (4). Dr. Brown was indicted for overcharging Medicare patients in the form of (a) billing for unperformed services, (b) performing and billing for medically unnecessary tests and services, (c) double-billing for medical services, and (d) upcoding. The government supported its allegations with little more than ten sworn declarations from insurance carrier employees and patients, accompanied by statistical and documentary evidence.

Even association with corporate entities will not protect the unwary physician. Dr. John Lorenzo (5) owned a corporation that in turn owned a dental clinic doing business as "U.S. Mobile." The clinic billed for oral cancer screenings, as a consultant had advised, submitting 3,783 claims at a rate of $50 per examination to Medicare through Pennsylvania Blue Shield and receiving $130,719.10. The court held that Dr. Lorenzo knew the checkups billed as oral cancer examinations were not covered without a referral from a physician, and that he had acted with reckless disregard of the truth or falsity of the information submitted. The government pierced the corporate veil under the theory that the enterprise was merely Dr. Lorenzo's alter ego. As a result, Dr. Lorenzo and the business entity were held jointly and severally liable and compelled to pay three times the amount of damages ($130,719.10 × 3 = $392,157.30). He was also required to pay an additional civil penalty of not less than $5,000 for each false claim. In sum, Dr. Lorenzo was ordered to repay $19,307,157.

Courts are officially accepting "reckless disregard" and "deliberate ignorance" to fulfill the intent element in proving criminal conduct. In fact, a Michigan appeals court ruled that the Medicaid False Claims Act and the Health Care False Claims Act are both constitutional and do not require proof of criminal intent (6) (the lower court had ruled that "innocent behavior" could not be a crime because "corrupt intent" was a necessary element). If the Michigan court's ruling stands, it will be a major change in the intent requirement in criminal behavior.

The False Claims Act encourages whistleblowing by protecting employees from being discharged, demoted, suspended, threatened, harassed, or discriminated against.* The government may seize any assets related to the alleged fraud while an investigation is pending, and under *Savran* (7) it is up to the physician (not the government) to show the court what is untainted among the seized funds or property. Thus, even if a doctor is eventually vindicated, his or her practice may suffer under the mere suspicion of fraudulence.

---

*If any of the above actions are taken against the whistleblower, the False Claims Act requires that he or she be reinstated with seniority, double back pay with interest, and compensation for special damages, attorney's fees, and the cost of litigation. The whistleblower does not have to pay taxes on any award, because it is considered a restoration of what he or she has lost.

Targeted Area: Billing

There are many ways in which a patient's treatment can be misinterpreted or mischaracterized to the payor, among them billing for services that are unperformed or performed without proper documentation as to their necessity; unbundling and fragmentation, whereby services billed together at a set price are also billed again separately; and code creep, or billing for more expensive services than were performed. In fairness, however, it should be said that the rules are so complicated that physicians and office managers alike may be left to guess at the correct billing codes for all the procedures performed in the office.

The new Evaluation and Management Guidelines proposed by HCFA are tied to the three key components of evaluation and management around which the work component of the physician payment system was structured: the extent of the history, the extent of the examination, and the complexity of the medical decision making. The guidelines are complex, burdensome, and sometimes arbitrary. Although the guidelines were not implemented in July 1998, as HCFA threatened, they will be at some point, and that may result in the denial of 50% of claims for lack of documentation. Another concern is that honest mistakes in documentation are going to be regarded as fraudulent. For instance, the common practice of bringing surgical patients to the hospital the day before surgery for laboratory tests would be considered unbundling under the diagnosis-related group (DRG) reimbursement rules, which state that if these tests occur within 72 hours of the surgery, they are bundled into the DRG reimbursement for the surgery. Eighty percent of the hospitals in the United States are guilty of this crime, which is being vigorously prosecuted.

Targeted Area: Employer-Employee Relationship

In *Williams v Good Health Plus, Inc.* (8), the court found that a corporation could not legally practice medicine and therefore could not be held liable for malpractice. However, hospitals and health maintenance organizations (HMOs) are liable for improper oversight of care, failure to properly review credentials and expertise, improper credentialing and privileging, and failure to protect patients from malpractice of physicians when the entity knew or should have known that malpractice was likely (9). Hospitals and HMOs may have a nondelegable duty to select and retain only competent physicians (10).

Even if there is no negligence on their part, employers may still be liable under the doctrine of *respondeat superior* for the negligence of employees acting within the scope of their employment. Problems generally arise from trying to pinpoint exactly when a physician is acting within the scope of his or her employment. Are physicians independent contractors or employees of HMOs and hospitals? Although one staff-model HMO was found liable for the negligence of its physicians (11), nonstaff- and independent staff association–model HMOs are in a different situation. Case law would suggest that *respondeat superior* applies to an HMO or hospital if the patient is seen on its premises (12), but not if the patient is seen at the doctor's office.

Teaching physicians and institutions may run into trouble if they bill for services rendered by residents, medical students, and fellows without establishing a relationship between the patient and an attending physician. This means that the teaching physician must personally examine the patient, confirm the diagnosis, revise the diagnosis, determine the course of treatment, and be present in the room during any treatment or procedure. The University of Pennsylvania and the University of Virginia hospitals were heavily fined for not adhering to these guidelines. It is unlawful for one physician to allow another physician whose license has been suspended or revoked to hold clinics, act as a house physician, and then submit bills under the first physician's name. This amounts to collecting fees under false pretenses. Similarly, it is also illegal for physician's assistants, nurse practitioners, and nurses to bill for procedures that they are not licensed to perform.

Targeted Area: Referrals

If doctors were to refer patients in expectation of payment, instead of in response to a patient's need for services, it is likely that the cost of care would be greatly inflated, and that instead of receiving the best care available, patients would be referred to the highest bidder. The Anti-Kickback Act bars the giving or receiving of anything of value directly or indirectly (more than $300 per year) to induce or solicit referrals (13). The public policy reason for applying this stringent rule to physicians when it is not applied to other professions is to eliminate incentives to overuse medical services. In 1986, Congress amended the Anti-Kickback Act to close loopholes and broaden its coverage.

In *Inspector General v Hanlester Network* (14), an administrative law judge held that to violate Section 1128B(b)(2) a party must knowingly offer to pay remuneration that is conditional on the recipient agreeing to refer patients (quid pro quo). Mere investment in a business venture in which payments are offered or made in the hope that a provider would be encouraged to refer patients is not enough. However, excessive compensation may prove a violation of the act. In *United States v Kensington Hospital* (15), in which physicians made substantial contributions to the Kensington building fund in exchange for exclusive hospital-based service contracts, the court held that this was an issue of fact that a jury should decide. In *United States v Greber* (16), the owner of a Holter monitoring company (Cardio-Med) made an arrangement with a certain cardiologist who agreed to use the company's monitors on his patients in return for 40% of the money Cardio-Med received for the service. On these facts, the court ruled that even if only part of the payment was made to induce referrals, both Cardio-Med and the cardiologist were guilty of participating in a kickback scheme.

Eventually, hospitals will have to examine whether the antikickback rules apply to offering food and drinks to physicians in a special lounge, free parking, cut-rate rent for office space, and interest-free loans. One of the charges against Columbia Health Care Associates, for example, was that they offered doctors silent partnerships, ostensibly in return for referring patients to their facilities. What if payments made to a physician for the sale of his or her practice were interpreted as remuneration for referral of patients to a hospital?

The Stark Bill (17) prohibits physicians from referring patients to entities in which the referring physician has a financial interest. It was passed when studies revealed that 25% of laboratories were owned by physicians, and that patients referred to clinical laboratories in which the referring doctor had a financial interest received 45% more laboratory services (18). Referrals affected by the Stark Bill include, in addition to laboratory services, physical therapy, occupational therapy, radiology, durable medical equipment/supplies, parenteral and enteral nutrients/supplies, prosthesis, orthotics, prosthetic devices/supplies, home health care, and outpatient prescription drugs. The law will attribute ownership to physicians if services are owned by their spouses, parents, brothers and sisters, children, grandparents, in-laws, or business partners, or even by physicians to whom they refer patients.

NEGLIGENCE

For a physician to be liable to patients for malpractice, the plaintiff must prove all the elements of negligence: (a) that the physician had a duty toward the patient, (b) that the physician breached that duty, (c) that the breach caused the damage, and (d) that there was demonstrable damage.

For a duty to exist between a patient and a provider, a relationship must exist. Problems arise in pinpointing the moment this relationship is formed. A written contract is not necessary; the relationship is usually established when the physician examines the patient. There are a few modern-day exceptions, however. Most common is the physician who is paid a capitated fee to take care of patients assigned by a managed care organization. Under normal circumstances, physicians in these arrangements will wait for the patients to whom they are assigned to initiate contact. If a doctor collects a capitated payment for a substantial period without initiating contact with the patient, however, scholars believe that the doctor may be liable for failing to detect conditions that develop during that time.

A patient may continue to think of a certain physician as his or her doctor even though the patient has not been to see the doctor in more than 5 years, has not paid overdue bills, did not comply with the recommended regimen, and did not keep appointments. If a jury finds that a patient-doctor relationship existed, the physician is potentially liable for the preventive education that the patient should have received. It is wise, therefore, to establish a beginning and an end for patient contacts. Send a registered letter to patients whom you consider out of your practice, advising them that you are no longer responsible for their care.

If a relationship exists, the physician must anticipate the medical needs of his or her patients and advise them on reasonable and prudent steps for maintaining their health. This is referred to as *the duty of continuing care* (19), or *anticipatory guidance.* In other words, the physician has a duty to provide good advice and timely care (vaccines; recommendations to stop smoking, to exercise, or to eat a prudent diet; information about the early warning signs of heart attack; etc.). The physician also has a duty to keep patient information confidential (20). Some states require affirmative duties, such as reporting child and spouse abuse to legal authorities, threats to potential victims, and human immunodeficiency virus infection to the sexual partners of patients.

CONSENT

Because patients have a constitutional right to exercise control over their bodies, touching them without appropriate permission is battery. Adult patients of sound mind are entitled to decide whether and when to submit to treatment, and they must be told all the risks and hazards of accepting or not accepting any proposed treatment as well as whether the physician has a financial interest in any of the proposed treatment options. But problems inevitably arise, because full disclosure is impossible (e.g., if it is not possible to inform the patient of every conceivable or inconceivable contingency).

ENFORCEMENT

Private Health Insurers

Although all health insurance companies have antifraud personnel, Empire Blue Cross and Blue Shield (New York) is perhaps the most aggressive in its efforts to ferret out fraudulent claims. In the past, insurers simply passed losses from fraud on to policy holders. As competition heated up and policy-holding employers balked, Blue Cross decided to fight fraud instead. In 1996, Blue Cross reported the recovery of $36.1 million, or 1% of gross revenues. Other insurers are likely to follow suit.

The Government's Arsenal

In addition to scrutinizing medical records, the U.S. Department of Justice now has hotlines (800-HHS-TIPS) that will accommodate anyone wanting to report suspected fraudulent conduct. Customary practices include interviewing present and past patients about the services they received for comparison to what the provider billed for and even sending patients undercover. The typical ploy is for a healthy investigator to obtain cosmetic services and then wait to see what the doctor bills for—illegal activities include providing weight loss advice but billing for hypertension treatment and performing hair replacement but billing for acne surgery or another covered service.

WHEN THE INVESTIGATOR ARRIVES

It is vital to understand the rights that physicians have when they are investigated for health care fraud. Doctors must cooperate with warrants, but can make it clear that they are not giving permission for search or seizure. Ask the person in charge if the requested documents can be delivered; sometimes this can be arranged. Call your lawyer and ask him or her to make a house call. Ask the person in charge to wait for your lawyer before proceeding with the search. Write down the names of all the agents on site, as well as of whoever signed the warrant—this will help your lawyer prepare your defense. Although it may be obstruction of justice to instruct staff not to talk to the agents, you can close the office and send the staff and patients home. Do not attempt to destroy or hide any documents. If you have recording instruments on hand, record the event (camera, video, or audio). Be careful, however, that you do not produce evidence of wrongdoing on your part. Investigators will want to copy everything on your computer, but you have the right to back up your files before the agents proceed, because they may damage your computer system.

IF A GOOD NIGHT'S SLEEP IS IMPORTANT

There are some protective measures that physicians can take. Develop a compliance program, and designate a compliance officer with the authority to say no. Automated risk integrity systems can be purchased that will monitor billing. Identify a "just in case" attorney, and pay a retainer to assure that he or she will be available if agents show up at your door. Conduct an outside audit—an objective party can identify potential problems that will not show up on internal audits. One valuable procedure is to compare your charges against a national average for your specialty. If you are more than one standard deviation from the mean, you will most likely be audited; this is monitored very closely.

Although it is not expected that all physicians will go to law school, it is prudent to follow the most recent health fraud cases and read the most recent government regulations. You should know the rules that apply to physicians and to your specialty.

Keep good records. This is your best protection. The new regulations will serve you in this regard, because it is now required that physicians keep detailed records of all patient-doctor transactions. It should be obvious by now that though it may be frustrating, oppressive, and bewildering to practice medicine with conscious attention to the law, it must be done. There are few medical options into which some regulation does not intrude, interfering with and placing limits on what physicians are allowed to do. The monitoring systems that are in place are sophisticated and predictable. The percentage of physicians being prosecuted increased 96% between 1996 and 1997 and will continue to increase.

Patients are now empowered with more knowledge about medicine and are more likely than ever to assert newfound rights. Once a malpractice suit, a *qui tam* action, or a government investigation is in place, the physician can achieve at best a Pyrrhic victory, prevailing in the legal action but losing his or her peace of mind, valuable time, resources, and reputation. Rather than viewing the law with fear and loathing, however, with practice, patience, and perseverance, physicians can learn to reduce the conflicts between law and medicine and to practice in greater harmony with the law, ethics, and professional standards. Society has shifted the focus of health care toward preventive medicine; a little preventive law is also good medicine.

REFERENCES

1. Gallup poll. Who do you trust? 1996.
2. Hirsh M, Klaidman D. The federal probe of Columbia/HCA is just part of a broad assault on health care fraud. *Newsweek* 1997;Aug 11:42.
3. Pomerance P. What do you do when the agents come? NHLA Seminar Materials. West Group, 1997:1.
4. *United States v Brown*, No. 92-3674 (1997 West Group).
5. *United States v Lorenzo*, No. 89-6933 (1997 West Group).
6. *Michigan v Motor City Hospital and Surgical Supply Inc.*, Mich Ct App, Nos. 19576, 196345, 12/13/97.
7. *United States v William Savran & Associates*, 755 F Supp 1165,1183 (ED NY 1991).
8. *Williams v Good Health Plus, Inc.*, 743 SW2d 373 (Tex Ct App 1987).
9. Hinden RA, Elden DL. Liability issues for managed care entities. *14 Seton Hall Leg J* 1990;1:7.
10. *Darling v Charleston Community Memorial Hospital*, 211 NE2d 253 (1965), cert denied, 383 US 946 (1966).
11. *Sloan v Metropolitan Health Council*, 516 NE2d 1104 (Ind Ct App 1987).
12. *Boyd v Albert Einstein Medical Center*, 547 A2d 1229 (Pa Super Ct 1988).
13. Anti-Kickback Act, 42 USC §1320a-1327b(b)(1).
14. Hanlester Laboratories (1991).
15. *United States v Kensington Hospital*, No. 90-5430 (March 14, 1991).
16. *United States v Greber*, 760 F2d 68 (3rd Cir 1985).
17. Stark Bill, 42 USC §1395nn(h)(6).
18. Financial arrangements between physicians and health care business. *Medical Care* 1994;32(2).
19. *Ricks v Budge*, 91 Utah 307 64 P2d 208 (1937).
20. *McDonald v Clinger*, 84 AD2d 482; 446 NY S2d 801 (1982).

7

Nutritional Factors in the Health of Minority Populations

Shiriki K. Kumanyika

Department of Human Nutrition and Dietetics, College of Health and Human Development Sciences, University of Illinois College of Medicine, Chicago, Illinois 60612

An examination of health profiles of African-Americans and other minority populations in the United States reveals a disproportionate need for attention to nutritional factors in these groups. In 1985, the six causes of death that accounted for major disparities in the health of minority populations (African-Americans, Hispanic Americans, American Indians and Alaska Natives, and Asian Americans and Pacific Islanders) when compared to whites were cardiovascular diseases, cancer, diabetes, infant mortality, cirrhosis of the liver, and injuries (Table 7-1) (1,2). These causes of death have multiple determinants, but nutrition interventions can substantially reduce risk in four of the six health problem areas. Three—cardiovascular diseases, cancers, and diabetes—relate to chronic diseases that are linked by compelling evidence to high-fat, high-salt, low-fiber dietary patterns and to the related epidemics of obesity and low physical activity levels (3,4). (The fourth, cirrhosis of the liver, is not linked to these factors.)

In contrast to the types of nutritional problems that stem from deficiencies in intake of energy, protein, or essential vitamins and minerals (or at the other extreme, to toxic intakes of micronutrients), chronic disease–related nutritional problems are thought to reflect slowly accumulating adverse effects of dietary patterns that have no identifiable short-term hazards. Nutritional issues in chronic disease can also be contrasted with medical nutrition problems—consequences of disease processes or organ failure—that command attention in acute care medicine (5). The nutritional issues involved in infant mortality relate to the more classic considerations of nutritional adequacy and the need for adequate weight gain during pregnancy. Yet maternal nutrition considerations are also connected, indirectly, to chronic disease. Among African-Americans, for example, in whom the risks of low birth weight are approximately double those for whites (6), concerns about infant health foster promotion of maternal weight gain even though excessive weight gain during pregnancy and postpartum retention of extra weight are risk factors for obesity.

To the extent that people can change what they eat, dietary factors that contribute to chronic diseases are potentially modifiable. McGinnis and Foege (4) have esti-

TABLE 7-1. *Causes of "excess" deaths in minority populations as identified by the Secretary's Task Force on Black and Minority Health*

Leading cause of death	Modifiable risk factors
Cardiovascular disease	Smoking High blood pressure High serum cholesterol Obesity
Cancers	Smoking Alcohol Environmental hazards
Homicide, suicide, and unintentional injuries	Alcohol and drug misuse Handgun availability
Diabetes	Obesity
Infant mortality	Low birth weight Maternal smoking Maternal nutrition First trimester of care Maternal marital status, age
Cirrhosis of liver	Alcohol

Adapted from ref. 1.

mated that as many as one in seven deaths can be attributed to diet and activity patterns, rendering nutrition and activity second only to tobacco (to which nearly one in five deaths can be attributed) as causes of preventable deaths. However, the potential for risk reduction through nutrition intervention has generally not been realized in the U.S. population as a whole and especially not in African-Americans (7–10) (Figs. 7-1 and 7-2). Relatively few Americans consume diets that meet the current guidelines (7) (Table 7-2), and the contribution of diet-related chronic diseases to the

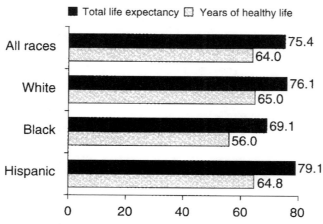

FIG. 7-1. Life expectancy and years of healthy life, United States: 1990. (From *Working for heart health in African-American communities.* National Heart Lung and Blood Institute, 1997, with permission.)

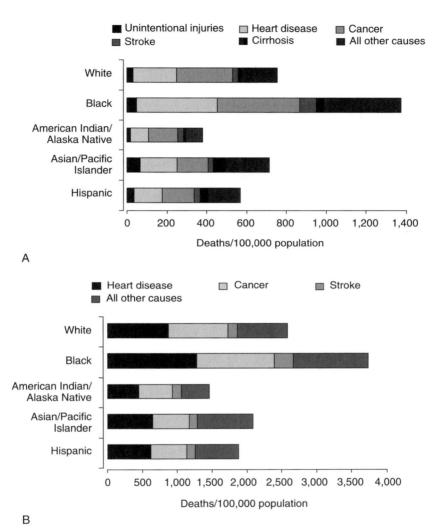

FIG. 7-2. A: Death rates for selected causes for persons 45 to 64 years of age by race and ethnic origin: United States, 1989–1991. **B:** Death rates for selected causes for persons 65 to 74 years of age by race and ethnic origin: United States, 1989–1991. (From National Center for Health Statistics, U.S. Vital Statistics, 1990, with permission.)

morbidity/mortality gap identified by the Task Force on Black and Minority Health continues. Due both to methodologic problems and a lack of appropriate data, the specific contribution of nutritional factors to the excess of deaths from chronic diseases in some minority communities has been difficult to quantify (e.g., whether African-Americans have diets higher in fat and salt or lower in fiber than whites or are more sensitive to the effects of these dietary factors at any given level of intake) (2,11). An excess of obesity and obesity-related diabetes is quite evident in most

TABLE 7-2. *Dietary guidelines for Americans*

Eat a variety of foods.
Balance the food you eat with physical activity—balance or maintain your weight.
Choose a diet with plenty of grain products, vegetables, and fruits.
Choose a diet low in fat, saturated fat, and cholesterol.
Choose a diet moderate in sugars.
Choose a diet moderate in salt and sodium.
If you drink alcoholic beverages, do so in moderation.

Adapted from ref. 22.

minority populations (12). It has been difficult to tie the excess of obesity to shorter life spans in minority populations, however, partly because of a lack of data and because evolution toward the full spectrum of chronic diseases in some minority populations is incomplete (13,14).

Physicians' lack of attention to nutritional issues has been cited as one major reason for the persistence of nutrition problems in society (15,16). Much of what is needed to effect population-wide dietary change takes place at the public policy level; however, in the media, community institutions, and private homes, physicians are, without question, gatekeepers (e.g., for referrals to dietitians or health educators) and key reference points for consumers with respect to personal health and health behavior. For example, in a survey of 20- to 50-year-old African-American and Hispanic American adults in Chicago, 48% of Hispanic Americans and 54% of African-Americans indicated that physicians were their primary sources of health-related information (17). This is somewhat ironic, given that the average physician may have only an intuitive sense of the relevance of nutrition to health.

The understanding and appreciation of nutritional factors have been grossly underspecified within the esoteric knowledge base of allopathic medicine (15,16). Nutrition is a uniquely integrative science that draws on core medical sciences, such as biochemistry and physiology, and links them to the environment. Nutrition-sensitive chronic diseases, such as cancer and cardiovascular diseases, are now commonly addressed in general medical practice (5,18), yet the cursory or absent coverage of nutrition in traditional medical school curricula is legendary and seems to be an intractable problem (16). One reason for the seeming incompatibility of nutrition and medicine may be the different placements of medical science (high status) and food and nutrition (low status) in the academic hierarchy. Even to suggest that the mundane issues of food selection and food preparation share the same domain as medical science may appear nonsensical to some physicians. This cultural bias may also influence the ability of physicians to yield territory to and appreciate health professionals who are trained in nutrition science and clinical nutrition (e.g., registered dietitians, physician clinical nutritionists). Another factor may be the dominance of the curative perspective in medicine. The curative medical perspective tends to focus somewhat narrowly on treating established disease, whereas health is defined more broadly as "a state of optimal physical, mental, and social well-being, and not merely the absence of disease and infirmity" (19). Nutrition and food, with the images they elicit of a nurturing mom in the kitchen, a sumptuous feast at celebrations, self-indulgence, and self-expression (20), fit easily into a definition of health that includes social well-being, but they become tangential, almost negative, concepts when viewed from the perspective of "medicine." If the definition of health is expanded to include prevention of diseases [as in holistic health, "a system of preventive medicine that takes into account the whole individual, his own responsibility for his well-being and the total influences—social, psychological, environmental—that affect health, including nutrition, exercise, and mental relaxation" (19)], then the distance from the purely curative medical perspective becomes even greater, and the relevance of nutrition and food becomes explicit.

PUBLIC HEALTH, EVOLUTIONARY, AND CONSUMER PARADIGMS FOR RELATING NUTRITION TO HEALTH

From a public health perspective, the potential for the foods people eat to confer risk or protection in relation to a wide range of health problems is well recognized, and avoidance of nutrition-related health problems is a major objective of U.S. national public health policies. Large sums are spent in support of ongoing national probability sample surveys to monitor the food supply, dietary intakes, and biochemical or physical nutritional status of the U.S. population and to evaluate the association of diet and nutrition variables with disease and death rates (7). From the array of nutrients and dietary constituents known to affect the various biochemical or metabolic pathways that could be considered, priorities are selected using a decision-making algorithm to categorize nutritional factors as current, potential, or not-current public health issues (Fig. 7-3). Given the range of choices available to an individual and the multitude of potentially healthful dietary patterns, this algorithm is an empirical way of determining which aspects of the way people eat, if any, are problematic.

In the public health algorithm, evidence from experimental or epidemiologic nutrition studies provides theoretical reference points for classifying intakes of various nutrients or dietary constituents as low (e.g., the Recommended Dietary Allowances) (21) or high (e.g., the U.S. dietary guidelines) (22). Objective health data for population subgroups with low or high intakes are then examined to determine whether there is definitive, suggestive, or no evidence of excess rates of disease or deaths in association with intake. Definitive evidence suggesting nutrition-related risks in an identifiable portion of the population constitutes a public health nutrition issue that can then be addressed by food regulatory policy (e.g., the long-standing practice of requiring enrichment of processed flour with iron and B vitamins, or recently instituted regulations requiring fortification of certain foods with folic acid to reduce the potential for birth defects). Suggestive evidence of nutrition-related risks is addressed with dietary guidance policy (e.g., advice to the public to consume less fat, less salt, more dietary fiber, and more fruits and vegetables to decrease their chances of developing cardiovascular diseases and cancers) (22). Dietary guidance may also be provided, with respect to nutrient or food intake levels that cannot be classified as too low or too high according to existing standards, if intakes are found to be associated with increased rates of diseases or death.

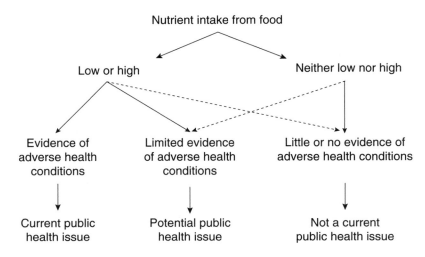

FIG. 7-3. Setting nutrition monitoring priorities. (From ref. 7, with permission.)

The public health paradigm of determining by observation which dietary patterns seem to be healthful or problematic is compatible with an evolutionary perspective on nutritional needs in which chronic illnesses are viewed as a mismatch between genes and environment. If one accepts the assumption, for which there is considerable evidence, that gene expression is sensitive to nutritional factors, then nutrition-related chronic diseases can be viewed as the consequences of having a genetic makeup that is geared for survival in one type of environment but that has, in a changed environment, become a liability. To quote Davies's thought-provoking discussion of this subject:

> It is reasonable to consider patients as individuals of the species *Homo sapiens sapiens*, whose genetic make up is that of hunter-gatherers, but who have been transposed into the modern 20th century environment with its attendant problems of extensive man-made pollution, the modern soil nutrient-deficient, contaminant rich supply, high-fat/sugar/protein low fibre diets and high stress, high tech life-styles. (18, p. 6)

In part, Davies is commenting on the longer, related text by Weatherall (23), who summarizes several possible examples of diseases that constitute "penalties we are paying for past evolutionary successes." Weatherall includes Neel's hypothesis that the dramatic increase in the prevalence of diabetes mellitus might be due to "dietary plenty superimposed on a thrifty genotype that had been selected to take advantage of sporadic food availability in primitive societies." Although the "thrifty genotype" as such has not been identified, the very high prevalence of diabetes, usually with accompanying obesity, in diverse populations, including American Indians, Pacific Islanders, and Asian Indians, and the moderately high prevalence in Hispanic Americans and African-Americans suggest that maladaptation to modernizing environments disproportionately affects populations that have recently experienced economic hardships and "feast or famine" conditions. The people who were really efficient at storing calories survived famine but were then biologically primed for a marked disadvantage in an environment characterized by the availability of calorie-dense food with greatly reduced opportunities for caloric expenditure through obligatory activity. Weatherall notes that Weiss has extended the thrifty genotype hypothesis to a "new world syndrome" in which obesity, gallstones, gallbladder cancer, and abnormalities of cholesterol metabolism may be caused by an underlying, possibly genetic abnormality of lipid metabolism that interacts with modern diet.

Davies also comments on the relevance to nutrition of "biochemical individuality" (18)—a concept that dates back to the observation of inborn errors of metabolism by Sir Archibald Garrod in the 1920s and 1930s. For example, some individuals have higher than average requirements for certain vitamins or an altered ability to tolerate certain naturally occurring amino acids. Inherited deficiencies in enzyme functioning may be responsible and may also explain why some species require different quantities of certain nutrients than other species. However, the phenotype associated with such predispositions will not emerge or can be suppressed on the basis of the dietary environment or the person's dietary intake. Within contemporary society, those who are most able to adapt, either by genetic constitution or by dietary exposures, are the least likely to be seen by physicians, whereas those who adapt only partly or not at all develop diseases (18).

Viewing chronic diseases as the results of an underlying inability to adapt to the environment does not imply that such diseases cannot be prevented or treated, but it illustrates how central nutritional factors may be in prevention and treatment. This perspective also underscores that the disease process might be very far along by the time the patient presents for treatment and, furthermore, that any treatment provided may be competing with disease-perpetuating factors in the individual's environment. In this scenario, although clinical medicine may still have a considerable amount to offer in restoring function or arresting further decline, the value of addressing predisposing factors, such as nutrition, before the process has advanced to the point of requiring medical treatment is also evident. Davies notes, "Preventive possibilities go only so far within the 1-to-1 doctor-patient relationship where the environmental challenges to adaptive physiology are under only partial control of the patient" (18, p. 7).

Consumer paradigms of food, nutrition, and health must also be considered because they shape the interactions of patients and physicians on nutrition issues. First and foremost, one must recognize the primacy of cultural and psychosocial factors in food choice (20). Food choices determine nutrient intakes, rather than the reverse. In *Tasting Food, Tasting Freedom*, anthropologist Sidney W. Mintz reminds us of the strong cultural component of eating:

> For us humans, then, eating is never a "purely biological" activity (whatever "purely biological" means). The foods eaten have histories associated with the pasts of those who eat them; the techniques employed to find, process, prepare, serve, and consume the foods are all culturally viable, with histories of their own. Nor is the food ever simply eaten; its consumption is always conditioned by meaning. (20, p. 7)

Whether we, as health professionals, can admit it, self-imposed or medically prescribed (e.g., "My doctor told me I can't have . . .") health motivations and prescriptions are subordinate to cultural and emotional influences on eating, as well as to practical factors such as food availability and convenience. Maintaining specific food choices and eating traditions and the freedom to make choices may be especially salient for populations that have experienced oppression. Mintz discusses the meaning of food in slavery:

> But freedom could also mean other things besides freedom from cruelty, sexual aggression, and exhausting labor, imposed by the will and sadism of the master class. It could mean being free to move about, to marry, to choose one's work. It also could mean freedom to choose one's friends, one's clothing, and yes—even one's food. (20, p. 34)

Consumer perceptions about the roles of food in health clearly overlap with those of health professionals but may include an additional mix of folk beliefs, homeopathic concepts and misconceptions about allopathic concepts, and reactions to the emerging diet and health findings that seem to be reported almost daily in the news (15,24,25). Consumer perceptions of diet and health may reflect historical nutrition adequacy guidance (e.g., advice to eat sufficient high-protein foods or liver, or to use iodized salt), some of which conflicts with the dietary pattern now recommended (see Table 7-2). Consumer dietary practices may also include a variety of home remedies and self-prescribed treatments with foods and dietary supplements (26) that compete both behaviorally and psychologically with remedies prescribed by physicians.

IMPLICATIONS

The literature on consumer nutrition awareness and nutrition interventions suggests that substantial numbers of individuals are motivated to change their dietary patterns for health reasons and that such dietary changes are indeed possible in the types of special community and clinical settings represented in published research. Although the database on dietary interventions in ethnic minority populations is small, the potential for successful risk reduction through dietary intervention appears to apply to minority populations as well as to whites. For example, in a high-profile study (Dietary Approaches to Stop Hypertension) that reported large decreases in blood pressure among men and women who consumed a diet low in fat and high in fruits and vegetables and dairy products (27), two-thirds of the participants were African-Americans. Some trials have suggested that the same behavioral treatment programs result in less weight loss among African-American than in white participants (28). However, the blood pressure–lowering results in these trials have been similar for African-Americans and whites. Although these studies were not designed specifically to compare intervention effect sizes in African-Americans and whites, they do suggest that one should not necessarily be discouraged from attempting interventions in African-American populations because of concerns about problems with adherence. Similar effectiveness of sodium reduction for primary prevention of hypertension in African-Americans and whites was reported from the Trials of Hypertension Prevention (29).

A trial of CARDES (an audiovisual nutrition education program) as an aid to lipid lowering in African-Americans reported an 8% reduction in total cholesterol in African-American men and women who used the program to supplement office-based nutrition counseling over a 1-year period. The audiovisual program was specially designed to be usable by men and women with a range of literacy skills (reading at the fifth- to eighth-grade level or above), and worked equally well in participants with literacy scores at the fifth- to eighth-grade level or above (30). Agurs-Collins et al. (31) have provided an example of modest success of a weight reduction and exercise intervention for management of type 2 diabetes in a sample of older African-Americans.

As a first step in bringing the potential for reducing risks of nutrition-related diseases to bear on minority populations, physicians must recognize and accept that dietary advice and interventions can influence health problems they see on a day-to-day basis and to understand that the most powerful time to initiate this influence is early in the disease process, with attention to nutrition continuing on a permanent basis. The more difficult second step will be deciding what type of interventions to offer or promote. Individual-level interventions in which counseling attempts to foster and sustain healthful dietary behaviors against a continuing barrage of societal forces that promote unhealthful behaviors can be expected to meet with limited success, even when conducted by trained dietitians or health educators. Public health solutions that can address contextual factors in the food and nutrition environment and that measure their effectiveness in whole populations are clearly needed, but to become directly involved with these may seem inappropriate even for the primary care physician, who is trained to care for people one-on-one, and more far-fetched for specialists. To advocate for and reinforce public health advice as part of clinical encounters is the least that can be done (32). The physician who starts collaborative efforts with health care professionals who specialize in and address nutrition issues will be more effective. However, it may be that the entire face of medical practice will have to change before nutrition diseases of maladaptation can be appropriately addressed. Such changes could be driven by bottom-line considerations in a capitated system; for example, if there is a fixed amount of money for each insured individual, it costs less to keep the individual healthy than to treat the various diseases that he or she may develop over his or her life span. That the managed care revolution will follow a sufficiently rational trajectory to arrive at this big-picture, long-term view is something to hope for.

REFERENCES

1. US Department of Health and Human Services. *Report of the secretary's task force on black and minority health. Volume 1. Executive summary.* Washington: US Government Printing Office, 1985.
2. Kumanyika SK. Diet and nutrition as influences on the morbidity/mortality gap. *Ann Epidemiol* 1993;3:154–158.
3. Committee on Diet and Health, Food and Nutrition Board, Commission on Life Sciences, National Research Council. *Diet and health: implications for reducing risk of chronic disease.* Washington, D.C.: National Academy Press, 1989.
4. McGinnis JM, Foege WH. Actual causes of death in the United States. *JAMA* 1993;270:2207–2212.

5. van Weel C. Morbidity in family medicine: the potential for individual nutritional counseling. An analysis from the Nijmegen Continuous Morbidity Registration. *Am J Clin Nutr* 1997;65[Suppl]: 1928–1932.
6. National Center for Health Statistics. *Health United States, 1994.* Department of Health and Human Services publication no. PHS 95-1232. Hyattsville, MD: Public Health Service, 1995.
7. Federation of American Societies for Experimental Biology, Life Sciences Research Office. *Third report on nutrition monitoring in the United States. Executive summary.* Prepared for the Interagency Board for Nutrition Monitoring and Related Research. Washington: US Government Printing Office, 1995. Available at http://www.cdc.gov/nchswww/nchshome.html or http://www.nalusda.gov/fnic.html.
8. American Cancer Society. *Cancer facts and figures—1997.*
9. American Heart Association. *Heart and stroke: statistical update—1997.*
10. National Diabetes Data Group. *Diabetes in America,* 2nd ed. Washington, D.C.: National Institutes of Diabetes, Digestive, and Kidney Diseases, 1995.
11. Kumanyika SK. Racial and ethnic issues in diet and cancer epidemiology. In: Jacobs M, ed. *Diet and cancer: markers, prevention, and treatment.* New York: Plenum Press, 1994:59–70.
12. Kumanyika SK. Obesity in minority populations: an epidemiologic assessment. *Obes Res* 1994;2: 166–182.
13. Kumanyika SK, Golden PM. Cross-sectional differences in health status in U.S. racial/ethnic minority groups. Potential influence of temporal changes, disease, and lifestyle transitions. *Ethn Dis* 1991; 1:50–59.
14. Gillum RF. The epidemiology of cardiovascular disease in black Americans. *N Engl J Med* 1996;335:1597–1599.
15. Truswell S. Nutritional attitudes and practices of primary care physicians. *Am J Clin Nutr* 1997; 65:6S.
16. Tobin BW. Nutrition in the basic medical sciences curriculum: an introduction to generalist physician training through problem-based learning. *Nutr Today* 1997;32:54–62.
17. Kumanyika S, Savage D, Ramirez AG, et al. Beliefs about high blood pressure prevention in a sample of black and Hispanic adults in Chicago. *Am J Prev Med* 1989;5:21–26.
18. Davies S. Scientific and ethnical foundations of nutritional and environmental medicine. Part II. Further glimpses of "the higher medicine." *J Nutr Environ Med* 1995;5:5–11.
19. *Dorland's illustrated medical dictionary,* 28th ed. Philadelphia: WB Saunders, 1994:736.
20. Mintz SW. *Tasting food, tasting freedom: excursions into eating, culture and the past.* Boston: Beacon Press, 1997.
21. Subcommittee on the tenth edition of the RDAs, Food and Nutrition Board, Commission on Life Sciences, National Research Council. *Recommended dietary allowances,* 10th ed. Washington, D.C.: National Academy Press, 1989.
22. US Department of Agriculture, US Department of Health and Human Services. *Nutrition and your health: dietary guidelines for Americans,* 4th ed. Washington: US Government Printing Office, 1995.
23. Weatherall D. The role of nature and nurture in common diseases: Garrod's legacy. *J Nutr Environ Med* 1995;5:63–76.
24. Buttriss JL. Food and nutrition: attitudes, beliefs, and knowledge in the United Kingdom. *Am J Clin Nutr* 1997;65[Suppl]:1985–1995.
25. van Woerkum CMJ. Media choice in nutrition education of general practitioners. *Am J Clin Nutr* 1997;65[Suppl]:203–205.
26. Commission on Dietary Supplement Labels. *Report of the Commission on Dietary Supplement Labels.* November 1997.
27. Appel LJ, Moore TJ, Obarzanek E, et al. A clinical trial of the effects of dietary patterns on blood pressure. *N Engl J Med* 1997;336:1117–1124.
28. Kumanyika SK. The impact of obesity on hypertension management in African Americans. *J Health Care Poor Underserved* 1997;8(3):365–378.
29. Kumanyika SK, Hebert PR, Cutler JA, et al. Feasibility and efficacy of sodium reduction in the trials of hypertension prevention, phase I. *Hypertension* 1993;22:504–512.
30. Kumanyika SK, TenHave T, Adams-Campbell L. Cholesterol reduction in African Americans given "CARDES" take-home instruction to supplement dietitian counseling. *Ethn Dis* 1997;7:S7.
31. Agurs-Collins TD, Kumanyika SK, TenHave TR, Adams-Campbell LL. A randomized controlled trial of weight reduction and exercise for diabetes management in older African-American subjects. *Diabetes Care* 1997;20(10):1503–1511.
32. Mant D. Effectiveness of dietary intervention in general practice. *Am J Clin Nutr* 1997;65[Suppl]: 1933–1938.

8

Management of Hypertension in Minorities

Richard Allen Williams

Department of Medicine, University of California, Los Angeles, UCLA School of Medicine, Los Angeles, California 90024, and Minority Health Institute, Inc., Beverly Hills, California 90211

This chapter on hypertension has been included to emphasize the importance of the disease and that it must be better understood and correctly treated if its toll on life and health is to be diminished. High blood pressure affects approximately 50 million people in the United States—almost one-fifth of the population, more than enough to justify calling it an epidemic. It prompts more visits to doctors' offices and more writing of prescriptions than any other disease (1) and is estimated to have cost the nation more than $23 billion dollars in 1995 in medicines, health services, and loss of productivity (2).

Despite extensive efforts to control hypertension, beginning with the federally sponsored National High Blood Pressure Education Program (NHBPEP) instituted in 1972 (3), and despite the acquisition of informative epidemiologic data from landmark studies such as the National Health and Nutrition Examination Surveys (NHANES I, II, and III) (4), as well as other key investigations, the disease is far from under control. Figures from the sixth Joint National Committee Report (JNC VI) indicate that only approximately 27% of those under treatment for high blood pressure are at goal blood pressure levels (5). The wide disparity between effort and outcome can be interpreted in many ways, but the way physicians approach management of this disease is a significant part of the problem. This chapter focuses on how health practitioners' management of hypertension can be optimized to increase control over the disease. Special populations—black patients in particular—are used to illustrate how a change from a general, global approach to treatment, in which it is assumed that one size fits all, to a more individualized, culturally sensitive model may have a positive impact on the results.

HYPERTENSION IN BLACKS

Hypertension is not an equal-opportunity killer. Although high blood pressure affects both genders and all races, cultures, ethnic groups, and ages, it does so in a disproportionate manner. For instance, blacks demonstrate higher blood pressure levels than whites and have higher rates of overall mortality with the disorder than others. According to data from NHANES III, of the 50 million adults with hypertension in the United States, 32% are black, even though only 12% of the population is black (4). Ofili (6) notes that blacks have earlier onset, greater prevalence, and greater severity of the disease, resulting in a fivefold increase in the risk of fatal stroke and end-stage renal disease and a doubling of the risk of death from heart disease. Obviously, there is a control gap between blacks and whites in the outcomes of antihypertensive management. Although no one can say definitively why this disparity exists, it is appropriate to explore some of the factors that may contribute to it.

DIFFERENCES IN PATHOPHYSIOLOGY BETWEEN BLACK AND WHITE HYPERTENSIVES

For reasons that have been speculated on by many but determined as yet by none, there are several notable differences in the pathophysiologic manifestations of hypertension in whites and blacks.

Psychosocial Stressors

Several excellent studies, including those by Harburg et al. (7), have documented a strong link between psychosocial stress and hypertension. The effects of psychosocial stressors can now be measured in physical and hemodynamic terms, making it clear that factors such as socioeconomic status, environment, anxiety, frustration, and depression must be included in the pathogenetic lexicon of hypertension. Probably less attention has been paid to the role psychosocial factors play because they have come on the scene more recently in the phylogeny than physical parameters such as hemodynamic variables. Eliot aptly points out [as noted in Williams (8)] that there have been approximately 1,600 generations of humans, but only 300 generations that have lived outside of caves and interacted with the environment and each other in a societal manner. Thus, fight-or-flight responses measurable in physical terms have been more typical of humans over the majority of history than have mental or psychological reactions. As life has become more complex and interactive, however, psychosocial stressors have come increasingly into play. This is especially true of blacks in America, in whom psychosocial stressors have been found to cause an increase in blood pressure. James (9) refers to the coping mechanisms that blacks develop to handle such stress as "John Henryism," a term adopted from a folk legend about a black railroad laborer who won an epic "man versus machine" battle with a steam drill but dropped dead from exhaustion.

Neurogenic Factors

An extensive body of research has demonstrated that certain nervous system events elicit responses in the cardiovascular system. The catecholamines, elaborated by the adrenal medulla and present in the sympathetic nervous system, should be considered part of the neurogenic mechanisms of hypertension. There is evidence that hypertensive blacks possess lower levels of plasma dopamine beta-hydroxylase (10); this may be related to renal defects and implies decreased sympathoadrenal tone. Much more research is needed and warranted in this intriguing area.

Cardiac and Hemodynamic Parameters

Since the landmark 1955 report by Perrera on end-stage organ damage caused by hypertension, numerous studies have corraborated that hypertension causes left ventricular hypertrophy (LVH), coronary artery disease, and congestive heart failure. Although the pathogenic relationship between hypertension and the latter two complications has received much attention, LVH is only now receiving its due, thanks largely to pioneering work by Savage et al. (11). It is now clear that in assessing the cardiac and hemodynamic consequences of high blood pressure, we as physicians should know more than that blood pressure is the product of cardiac output and peripheral vascular resistance; we must also be aware of the risk gradient associated with the severity of increased left ventricular mass index as determined by echocardiography. Black patients appear to be more likely to develop LVH, which has been determined to be an independent risk factor for sudden death.

Renal Mechanisms

From a pathophysiologic standpoint, it is important to recognize that blacks exhibit more nephrosclerosis than do whites. This may be the cause of increased rates of renal insufficiency and end-stage renal disease in blacks. Increased sodium retention, and decreased potassium and kallikrein excretion are other characteristics of the altered renal state in black hypertensive patients (12). Although total peripheral resistance is similar in blacks and whites, renal vascular resistance is often higher in blacks and increases in proportion to systemic pressure. Thus, renal damage may progress at a quicker rate in blacks even though total peripheral resistance is no higher than in whites.

Vascular Mechanisms

Endothelial relaxation is now considered a key component of vascular reactivity, and some very significant racial differences have been observed (13). In general, the blood vessels of blacks tend not to relax as well as those of whites. The difference in vascular reactivity may be due in part to differences in levels of nitric oxide (NO), which has been found to be the principal endothelium-relaxing factor, and endothelin, a potent vasoconstrictor found in blood vessel walls. Blacks have been shown to have a reduced NO-dependent vasodilator activity during mental stress (14). In addition, increased levels of ET-1, the main endothelin produced by the endothelium, are found in blacks with familial hypertension (15).

Endocrine and Metabolic Factors

Hormones that show distinct racial profiles are renin, which tends to be lower in blacks [as demonstrated by Brunner et al. (16)], and endogenous renal vasodilators such as kinins, atrial natriuretic factor, prostaglandins, and dopamine. Hormonal differences appear to have unfavorable implications for the pathogenesis of high blood pressure in blacks, as well as for the use of antihypertensive drugs that inhibit the renin-angiotensin system (RAS).

Blacks tend to be salt-sensitive (i.e., they do not tolerate salt-loading as well as whites, and may respond to it by developing hypertension) (17). This implies a definite need for physicians to assist blacks in controlling their dietary intake of salt.

Cellular Parameters

Intriguing and important research has been conducted by Woods et al. (18) on the cellular mechanisms involved in the pathogenesis of hypertension. Elevated red-cell concentrations of sodium and calcium, decreased transmembrane sodium transport activity, and decreased active and passive sodium-potassium red-cell transport activity are found in both hypertensive blacks and their normotensive sons. This has prompted speculation that methods might be developed that would predict hypertension at the cellular level in normotensive persons, making prevention more feasible.

Obesity

The Framingham and Evans County studies documented that people who are 20% or more overweight have two to three times the risk of developing high blood pressure. A strong correlation has also been found between obesity and hypertension, particularly in black women. Thus, there is a positive association between ponderosity and blood pressure that is involved in the pathogenesis of hypertension. The insulin resistance syndrome (1), in which obesity, hypertension, diabetes mellitus, and dyslipidemia are seen together, is a perfect example of a medical situation that is best controlled by nonpharmacologic and pharmacologic therapy in unison.

Dietary Factors

Dietary factors include issues such as the effects of dietary intake of calcium, elaborated on by McCarron et al. (19) and others; potassium deficiency, studied by Langford et al. (20), who found a lower intake of this essential electrolyte in impoverished persons, especially blacks; and sodium intake, investigated by Dahl et al. (21), Miall and Oldham (22), and others as to its contribution to the pathogenesis of hypertension. These factors have been variously implicated in the high blood pressure seen in blacks, and must be studied further to elucidate the potential ramifications for the black population. According to Tobian et al. (23), hypokalemia causes thickening of the renal arteriolar intima; presumably, dietary increases in potassium can help to avert renal damage.

Genetics

Whether there are genes for hypertension and whether they occur disproportionately in blacks is uncertain at present. Also unknown is whether the angiotensin-converting

TABLE 8-1. *Pathophysiologic characteristics of hypertension in blacks*

Low cardiac output
Expanded plasma volume
Increased peripheral vascular resistance
Decreased renal blood flow
Increased salt sensitivity
Decreased plasma renin levels
Decreased sympathetic nervous function
Decreased natriuretic vasodilatory kinins and prostaglandins
Increased sodium-potassium ratio
Abnormal sodium-potassium cotransport and sodium-lithium countertransport
Abnormal cellular handling of calcium or magnesium

From Saunders E. Pharmacologic initiatives in black hypertensives. *ABC Digest Urban Cardiol* 1994;4:17–26, with permission.

enzyme (ACE) gene (24) is associated more often with hypertension in blacks than in whites, though there is evidence of an ACE gene deletion (as opposed to insertion) polymorphism that is believed to be functional in the etiology of hypertension in blacks. Table 8-1 shows some of the pathophysiologic factors important in black hypertensive patients.

This information on the pathophysiologic profile of hypertensive blacks supports individualization of antihypertensive treatments along racial lines. In other words, if it can be convincingly demonstrated that racial differences in the pathophysiology of the disease exist, then it seems logical to customize one's approach with race in mind. Certainly some disagree that a patient's racial group should be a determining factor in deciding drug therapy; however, it is difficult to ignore the compelling evidence that there are differences to which physicians must be attentive, though not oversensitive, if we are to provide the best, safest, most specific, and most effective treatment for our patients. Even those who disagree that there is a need for more racial consciousness in selecting drugs used in medical therapy for hypertension will agree that black patients have distinct characteristics and experience the ravages of the disease at an earlier age, with greater severity, and with more devastating complications than white patients. They will concede that because of the high prevalence, morbidity, and mortality rates from high blood pressure in blacks, it is necessary to be more aggressive in lowering their blood pressure to at least 130/85 mm Hg (perhaps even lower, if certain comorbid conditions, such as diabetes mellitus, are present) and to begin treatment earlier, in an attempt to forestall the carnage caused by the disease. It should be axiomatic that the principal goal is to reduce blood pressure as soon as possible and by any means necessary, as long as those means are reasonable and safe. Based on the facts reviewed and on the JNC VI objective of treating hypertension in a targeted manner, it makes sense to tailor antihypertensive medication to the patient in a manner that is sensitive to his or her individual characteristics, including race. In the following sections, I consider what the choices should be by looking at each of the major categories of antihypertensive medications and, based on the evidence, make recommendations for their use in treating black patients.

DIFFERENCES BETWEEN BLACK AND WHITE HYPERTENSIVE
PATIENTS IN RESPONSIVENESS TO DRUG THERAPY

Whether blacks and whites respond differently to the various classes of antihypertensive medication is a question frequently raised. One of the pivotal studies addressing this was the report by Materson et al. (25) in which the relative effectiveness of six drugs was compared in hypertensive black and white men. The study divided more than 1,200 men from 15 clinics into six treatment groups of approximately 200 subjects each and one smaller placebo group. This prospective, randomized, double-blind, placebo-controlled study that contained washout and titration phases provided significant results regarding differences between the two racial categories. A total of 1,292 men (48% black) with diastolic pressures ranging from 95 to 109 mm Hg and average baseline blood pressures of 152/99 mm Hg were assigned to receive either placebo or one of six drugs: the diuretic hydrochlorothiazide (12.5 to 50.0 mg per day), the beta blocker (BB) atenolol (25 to 100 mg per day), the ACE inhibitor captopril (25 to l00 mg per day), the central alpha-agonist (CAA) clonidine (0.2 to 0.6 mg per day), the calcium channel blocker (CCB) sustained-release diltiazem (120 to 360 mg per day), or the alpha-blocker (AB) prazosin (4 to 20 mg per day). The primary endpoint for the study was the achievement of goal blood pressure (diastolic pressure below 95 mm Hg) that was maintained after 1 year of treatment. The results demonstrated a statistically significant difference in the effectiveness of drug treatment on blacks and whites, with the CCB diltiazem being the most efficacious in black patients, and the ACE inhibitor captopril the least effective (Fig. 8-1). The authors of the study concluded that race (and age, to a lesser extent) exerted a powerful influence on the antihypertensive response to individual drug therapy.

A follow-up study was carried out by the same group, the Department of Veterans Affairs Cooperative Study Group on Antihypertensive Agents, to determine whether age-race subgroup or renin profile was the better predictor of blood pressure response to drug therapy. More than 1,100 men were the subjects for this trial. Notably, age-race subgroup significantly predicted the response of these patients to single-drug therapy, in contrast to renin profiling, which was only of borderline significance (26). Also important is the study by Saunders et al. (27) of the influence of race on blood-pressure response to antihypertensive medication, which compared the effects of three drugs—sustained-release verapamil, a CCB; atenolol; and captopril—in 394 blacks. Short-term decreases in diastolic blood pressure, similar to those observed in the study by Masterson, were noted, with the greatest response seen with the CCB. Other studies of comparative effectiveness include the Trial of Antihypertensive Interventions and Management, which analyzed the impact of diet combined with one of two drugs—either the diuretic chlorthalidone or the BB atenolol. Black patients showed a better response when treated with the diuretic and dietary intervention, whereas white patients responded more favorably to the alternative combination of atenolol with dietary intervention (28).

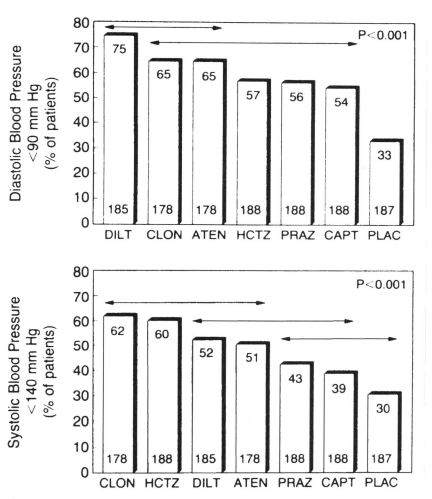

FIG. 8-1. Patients with a diastolic blood pressure of lower than 90 mm Hg or a systolic blood pressure of lower than 140 mm Hg at the end of the titration phase. The *P* values were derived by a chi-square test comparing the treatments. On the basis of pairwise comparisons, the horizontal arrows group drugs whose effects were not significantly different from the effects of other drugs under the same arrow but were significantly different from the effects of drugs not thus included. The numbers at the top of the bars indicate the percentage of patients with the response shown, and the numbers at the bottom of the bars indicate the number of patients in each group. ATEN, atenolol; CAPT, captopril; CLON, clonidine; DILT, diltiazem; HCTZ, hydrochlorothiazide; PLAC, placebo; PRAZ, prazosin. (From ref. 27, with permission.)

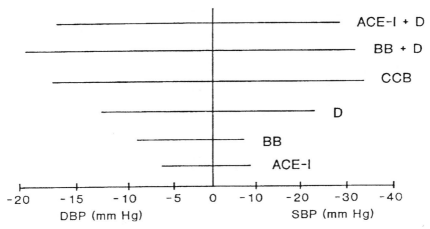

FIG. 8-2. Efficacy of four classes of antihypertensive drugs in hypertensive blacks. ACE-I, angiotensin-converting enzyme inhibitor; BB, beta blocker; CCB, calcium channel blocker; D, thiazide-type diuretic; DBP, diastolic blood pressure; SBP, systolic blood pressure. (From ref. 31, with permission.)

Based on data from a number of reports on the efficacy of various pharmacologic agents in hypertensive blacks, Hall and Kong (29) performed a small metaanalysis, represented in Fig. 8-2, which shows the average reduction in blood pressure with each of four classes of drugs: ACE inhibitors, diuretics, CCBs, and BBs. Overall, it was found that reduction of blood pressure in blacks was best achieved with either diuretics or CCBs when drugs from these classes were used as monotherapy. However, the diminished response to ACE inhibitors and BBs disappeared when drugs from these classes were used in conjunction with a diuretic.

Numerous reports of the relative ineffectiveness of ACE inhibitors and BBs when used as monotherapy in black patients have been presented in the literature, and the relative efficacy of the other four drug classes (diuretics, CCBs, ABs, CAAs) has been confirmed by various authors. It seems easily apparent that ACE inhibitors and BBs should not be used in blacks, and that treatment of blacks should be limited to the other four classes. However, the situation is not that simple. The dilemma is expressed best by Weir (30):

> Evaluation of the antihypertensive response to diuretics and calcium channel blockers compared to other drugs suggest [sic] that they may have an advantage in controlling blood pressure (BP). However, these comparative clinical trials have not assessed dietary salt consumption, the salt sensitivity status of the participants, nor have they explored full titration dosages of the comparative drugs. For these reasons, there is insufficient information to state with certainty whether some drugs may be more effective than others as monotherapy in controlling BP in hypertensives of African-American descent.

A similar opinion was expressed by Jamerson and DeQuattro (31):

> When compared to European Americans and other ethnic minorities, African Americans respond less favorably to beta-blockers and angiotensin-converting enzyme (ACE) inhibitors. Nevertheless, the observed response in African Americans to ACE inhibitors and beta-blockers is clinically significant . . . Ethnicity is not an accurate criterion for predicting poor response to any class of antihypertensive therapy. Thus, there is little justification to use racial profiling as a criterion for the avoidance of selected drug classes because of presumed lack of efficacy.

Messerli (32) goes further, saying, "The rationale for this selectivity is often speculative and has not been corroborated by any hard data. It is hoped that some of the prospective, randomized trials currently in progress will throw some light on this question." And Grimm et al. (33), who conducted the Treatment of Mild Hypertension Study (TOMHS), reflect thus on their results:

> It is commonly thought that there are important differences between African-Americans and Whites in blood-pressure lowering by type of drug. Specifically, African-Americans are frequently said to be especially responsive to diuretics and calcium channel blockers, and less responsive to beta-blockers and angiotensin converting enzyme inhibitors. However, in TOMHS, both ethnic groups responded well to all active drugs, and, although power is limited in TOMHS due to the relatively small number of African-Americans in each group, it is clear that both groups responded to all five drugs . . . the most striking finding in the TOMHS results is the similarity and homogeneity among African-Americans and Whites in terms of the management of hypertension.

These statements indicate that race is not an important factor in determining differences in blood-pressure manifestations. However, it is obvious that each of these authorities has given tacit or overt recognition to the fact that race must be considered in any serious approach to the treatment of black patients. There is no real conflict between these views and the concept of individualizing antihypertensive treatment according to race. All authorities agree that much more information is needed before strict racial profiling of therapy can be recommended, but data such as those from the Materson study indicate the direction in which we are moving. Other experts are calling for more individualization and more aggressive treatment of black patients. Meanwhile, meaningful information is expected to come from several prospective investigations that involve large numbers of black subjects being treated with a variety of antihypertensive agents. These studies include the Antihypertensive and Lipid Lowering Treatment to Prevent Heart Attack Trial and the African American Study of Kidney Disease and Hypertension Pilot Study, as well as studies that focus on the effectiveness of particular agents in the treatment of black hypertensives. An example of the latter type of study is the ABC Study of Hypertension, in which the new angiotensin receptor–blocker, candesartan cilexetil, is currently being administered to black patients. The results of this and other similar studies will, it is hoped, help identify the best drugs for use in treating the black hypertensive patient.

While these reports are awaited, it must be emphasized that the black hypertensive patient is at special risk (as has been stressed in the JNC VI report) and that every effort must be made to reduce that risk by both nonpharmacologic and pharmacologic means. In this regard, optimizing antihypertensive management for blacks includes using information on the pathophysiologic characteristics of hypertension in blacks and using available data on which drugs work best in this special population. Although it may not be possible to identify a "magic bullet," completely reliable, safe, and without troubling side effects—the drug *par excellence* for administration to black hypertensive patients—it is possible to improve on the generic approaches used in the past. Physicians must become better educated about therapeutic choices so that they can come closer to the ideal strategy for treating high blood pressure in blacks. An evidence-based approach to this extremely difficult problem is recommended, and, if aggressively carried out, should result in better control of hypertension and reduction in morbidity and mortality from this disease— a disease in which it is clear that race does indeed matter.

REFERENCES

1. Kaplan NM. *Clinical hypertension.* Baltimore: Williams & Wilkins, 1994.
2. Dustan HP, Roccella EJ, Garrison HH. Controlling hypertension. A research success story. *Arch Intern Med* 1996;156:1926–1935.
3. National Heart, Blood Vessel, Lung, and Blood Act of 1972. Pub L No. 92–423.
4. Burt VL, Whelton P, Rochella EJ, et al. Prevalence of hypertension in the US adult population. Results from the Third National Health and Nutrition Examination Survey, 1988–1991. *Hypertension* 1995;25:305–313.
5. Joint National Committee on Prevention, Detection, Evaluation and Treatment of High Blood Pressure. The sixth report of the Joint National Committee on Detection, Evaluation and Treatment of High Blood Pressure. *Arch Intern Med* 1997;157:2413–2446.
6. Ofili EO. Managing high blood pressure and hypertensive cardiovascular disease in blacks. *ABC Digest Urban Cardiol* 1995;2:20–25.
7. Harburg E, Erfurt JC, Hauenstein LS, Chape C, Schull WJ, Schork MA. Socio-ecological stress, suppressed hostility, skin color, and black-white male blood pressure: Detroit. *Psychosom Med* 1973;35:276–296.
8. Williams RA. The pathogenesis of hypertension: an overview. *J Hum Hypertens* 1990;4:69–71.
9. James SA, Keenan NL, Strogatz DS, Browning SR, Garrett JM. Socioeconomic status, John Henryism, and BP in black adults. *Am J Epidemiol* 1992;135:59–67.
10. O'Connor DT, Levine GE, Frigon RP. Homologous radio-immunoassay of human plasma dopamine-beta-hydroxylase: analysis of homospecific activity, circulating plasma pool and intergroup differences based on race, blood pressure and cardiac function. *J Hypertens* 1983;1:227–233.
11. Savage DD, Henry WL, Mitchell JR, et al. Echocardiographic comparison of black and white hypertensive subjects. *J Natl Med Assoc* 1979;71:709–712.
12. Warren SE, O'Connor DT. Does a renal vasodilator system mediate racial differences in essential hypertension? *Am J Med* 1980;69:425–429.
13. Dzau VJ, Gibbons GH, Morishita R, et al. New perspectives in hypertension research: potentials for vascular biology. *Hypertension* 1994;23:1132–1140.
14. Cardillo C, Kilcoyne CM, Cannon RO III, Panza JA. Racial differences in nitric oxide-mediated vasodilator responses to mental stress in the forearm circulation. *Hypertension* 1998;31:1235–1239.
15. Schiffrin EL. Endothelin: role in hypertension. *Biol Res* 1998;31:199–208.
16. Brunner HR, Sealey JE, Laragh JH. Renin subgroups in essential hypertension: further studies of their pathological and epidemiological characteristics. *Circ Res* 1973;32[Suppl]:99–109.
17. Falkner B, Kushner H. Effect of chronic sodium loading on cardiovascular response in young blacks and whites. *Hypertension* 1990;15:36–43.

18. Woods JW, Falk RJ, Pittman AW, Klemmer PJ, Watson BS, Namboodiri K. Increased red-cell sodium-lithium countertransport in normotensive sons of hypertensive parents. *N Engl J Med* 1982;306:593–595.

19. McCarron DA, Morris CD, Cole C. Dietary calcium in human hypertension. *Science* 1982;217:262–269.

20. Langford HG, Watson RL, Douglas BH. Factors affecting blood pressure in population groups. *Trans Assoc Am Physicians* 1968;63:135–146.

21. Dahl LK, Leitl G, Heine M. Influence of dietary potassium and sodium/potassium molar ratios on the development of salt hypertension. *J Exp Med* 1972;136:318–330.

22. Miall WE, Oldham PD. Factors influencing arterial pressure in the general population. *Clin Sci* 1958;17:409–444.

23. Tobian L, MacNeil D, Johnson MA, et al. Potassium protection against lesions of the renal tubules, arteries, and glomeruli and nephron loss in salt-loaded hypertensive Dahl S rats. *Hypertension* 1984;6[Suppl 1]:1–70.

24. Duru K, Farrow S, Wang JM, et al. Frequency of a deletion polymorphism in the gene for angiotensin converting enzyme is increased in African-Americans with hypertension. *Am J Hypertens* 1994;7:759–762.

25. Materson B, Reda DJ, Cushman WC, et al. Single drug therapy in men: a comparison of six antihypertensive agents with placebo. *N Engl J Med* 1993;328:914–921.

26. Preston RA, Materson BJ, Reda DJ, et al. Age-race subgroup compared with renin profile as predictors of blood pressure response to antihypertensive therapy. *JAMA* 1998;280:1168–1172.

27. Saunders E, Weir MR, Kong DW, et al. A comparison of the efficacy and safety of a beta-blocker, a calcium channel blocker and a converting enzyme inhibitor in hypertensive blacks. *Arch Intern Med* 1990;150:1707–1713.

28. Wassertiel-Smoller S, Oberman A, Blaufox MD, Davis B, Langford H. The Trial of Antihypertensive Interventions and Management (TAIM) study: final results with regard to blood pressure, cardiovascular risk, and quality of life. *Am J Hypertens* 1992;5:37–44.

29. Hall WD, Kong BW. Hypertension in blacks: nonpharmacologic and pharmacologic therapy. In: Saunders E, ed. *Cardiovascular diseases in blacks.* Philadelphia: FA Davis Co, 1991:145–169.

30. Weir MR. Population characteristics and the modulation of the renin-angiotensin system in the treatment of hypertension. *J Hum Hypertens* 1997;11(1):17–21.

31. Jamerson K, DeQuattro V. The impact of ethnicity on response to antihypertensive therapy. *Am J Med* 1996;101[3A]:22S–32S.

32. Messerli PH. Hypertension in special populations. *Med Clin North Am* 1997;81(6):1335–1345.

33. Grimm RH Jr, Grandits GA, Flack JM. Are black and white hypertensives really different? *ABC Digest Urban Cardiol* 1997;4:10–16.

9

Women's Health Issues

Anne L. Taylor

Department of Internal Medicine and Women's Health Programs, Department of Medicine, Division of Cardiology, Case Western Reserve University School of Medicine, Cleveland, Ohio 44106

In the past, "women's health" has meant reproductive and gynecologic health, areas in which women's health needs are clearly distinct from the health needs of men. In all other respects, women's health has not been considered notably different from men's health. Since the late 1980s, however, there has been increasing recognition that a significant knowledge gap exists in understanding the health needs of women, who represent more than one-half of the population. Although reproduction-related health is part of women's health, female gender is a significant modulating factor for areas of health common to both men and women, such as cardiovascular health, bone and joint health, neuropsychiatric health, nutrition, metabolism, and changes in health that occur throughout a life cycle. In addition, ethnically and culturally distinct groups of women may have very different health profiles and needs.

Examining causes of mortality in women further exposes the invalidity of the traditional equivalence of women's health with gynecologic health. Cardiovascular disease, cancer (non–gender-specific lung cancer causes more deaths in women than breast cancer), cerebral-vascular diseases, pneumonia, chronic lung disease, and accidental deaths are major causes of mortality in women. Disability in women is far more likely to be caused by nongynecologic diseases, such as osteoporosis and stroke, than by gynecologic diseases. The worldwide health consequences of human immunodeficiency virus (HIV) infection have assumed enormous importance among women, particularly women of color in this country and abroad.

Until the 1990s, clinical treatment decisions for many diseases highly prevalent in men and women were based on data from clinical research that concentrated on large cohorts of men, data that may not, therefore, be freely extrapolated to women. Thus, investigational efforts such as the National Institutes of Health (NIH)-funded Women's Health Initiative, which involved more than 152,000 women, and other studies designed to tease out the effects of gender, race, and culture on women's health are critical to narrowing the knowledge gap in women's health in the coming decades.

Concomitant with a new interest in researching the health-modulating effects of female gender is a heightened awareness that the practice of women's health care must evolve. Considering that childbearing years occupy only 40% of the average woman's lifespan, it is very clear that women's health care can no longer be simply reproduction-related but must include attention to cardiovascular health, bone and joint health, neuropsychiatric health, and nutritional needs throughout women's life cycles. To move away from women's health care that is delivered by caregivers who are focused only on reproduction-related health issues or who lack a generalized awareness of the special needs of women, a new model of health care delivery is needed, one that requires cross-disciplinary, collaborative efforts on the part of health care professionals.

To grasp the context for considering health issues particularly important to women, it is critical to understand the knowledge base underlying women's health, as defined by the National Academy on Women's Health Medical Education (1):

1. Knowledge of those conditions unique to women (e.g., gynecologic and obstetric conditions)
2. Knowledge of those conditions more common in women than in men (e.g., autoimmune diseases, depression, breast cancer)
3. Knowledge of those conditions with more serious impact for women than for men (e.g., osteoporosis)
4. Knowledge of those conditions that have manifestations, risk factors, interventions, or outcomes different in women than in men (e.g., coronary heart disease)
5. Knowledge of changes in women's health and wellness needs over women's life spans (e.g., nutritional requirements, body image changes, mood disorders associated with the reproductive-life cycle)

OVERVIEW OF MAJOR WOMEN'S HEALTH PROBLEMS

Cardiovascular Diseases

Coronary heart disease is an excellent model for emphasizing the effect of female gender on a cause of mortality that is highly prevalent in both men and women. Cardiovascular diseases kill more women annually than all forms of cancer, chronic lung disease, pneumonia, diabetes, and acquired immunodeficiency syndrome (AIDS) combined (2), yet the prevalence and consequences of heart disease in women continue to be underestimated by physicians and the lay population. It is widely believed that male gender is associated with susceptibility to cardiovascular morbidity and mortality and that female gender is associated with protection from cardiovascular disease. These generalizations are true for men and women in early adulthood, but they become progressively less relevant with each decade of life, so that by the seventh and eighth decades of life heart disease is equally prevalent in both sexes (2).

It is also apparent that female gender exerts a very powerful modulating effect on the disease, so much so that significant differences exist between men and women in the impact of risk factors promoting development of coronary atherosclerosis, in the presentation and clinical features of the disease, and in the morbidity and mortality of coronary events. The modulating effect of female gender may be positive or negative; it is true that women develop the disease approximately 10 years later than men, but when women experience a myocardial infarction, the outcome is substantially poorer than it is for men of similar age (2), and the disease is less likely to be aggressively managed.

Risk factors for coronary heart disease in women are generally the same as those in men: hypertension, diabetes mellitus, dyslipidemia, cigarette smoking, obesity, sedentary lifestyle, and family history. However, the impact of these risk factors on each gender differs. Diabetes mellitus increases the risk of developing coronary heart disease to a far greater extent in women than in men, and hypertriglyceridemia may be a more important risk factor in women than men (2,3). Reduction of cholesterol in women with established coronary heart disease has been shown to have substantial secondary preventive effects (2), but women with hypercholesterolemia tend to be undertreated. Cigarette smoking, a very potent risk factor, particularly for women taking oral contraceptives, has been increasing at higher rates among young women than among young men (3). The relationship of psychosocial factors, such as depression (five times more common in women than in men), gender-differentiated responses to stress, and the lesser social and economic support experienced by older women, to the development of coronary artery disease requires study (3).

Since the early 1990s, observational data have suggested that the risk of coronary heart disease is reduced by approximately 50% in women who take postmenopausal hormone replacement therapy (4,5). Although there are compelling biological effects of estrogen that would support a cardioprotective role for it, such as elevations in high-density lipoprotein cholesterol, reductions in low-density lipoprotein cholesterol and fibrinogen, and antiproliferative and antioxidant effects (as well as regulation of endothelial function) (6,7), the epidemiologic data that guide the use of estrogens have significant limitations (4,5). All studies to date have been observational or case-controlled, not interventional (4–7). Thus, significant differences in health profiles and behaviors exist between estrogen users (whether self-selected or otherwise) and controls in these studies (4,5). Postmenopausal estrogen users represent only approximately 15% of postmenopausal women and are overwhelmingly white, educated, upper middle–class women who display other health behaviors associated with decreased risk of coronary heart disease (8). Because of this, the true magnitude of the apparent benefit of estrogen use and its additive role in differences between risk factor profiles requires elucidation. There are no data on the effects of hormone replacement therapy in black women or women in other ethnic groups. Although estrogen may prove to be a very important cardiovascular therapeutic and preventive treatment for women, many more data are needed before specific guidelines for usage can be formulated.

Significant differences exist between men and women in the clinical features of coronary artery disease. In the Framingham study, myocardial infarction was the initial presentation in 43% of men versus 29% of women, whereas angina was the initial presentation in 26% of men versus 47% of women (9). The appearance of unstable angina and sudden death as initial presentations of coronary heart disease did not differ between the sexes. Anginal chest pain has less specificity in women as an indicator of significant coronary stenoses. Short- and long-term mortality after myocardial infarction have been shown to be significantly higher in women than in men (2,10).

Some factors that seem related to a poorer outcome for women with myocardial infarction than for men include older age at presentation, increased incidence of postinfarction angina, and congestive heart failure, as well as higher prevalences in women of diabetes and hypertension. Treatment patterns for men and women also differ; women are significantly less likely to undergo cardiac catheterization and revascularization procedures (2,3).

Cardiovascular disease is particularly important in black women. The mortality rate from cardiovascular disease is 69% higher in black women than in white women (2,10). Differences in the risk factor profiles of black and white women include greater prevalences in black women of hypertension, diabetes mellitus, obesity, and sedentary lifestyles. Significant differences in access to care, physicians' interpretation of symptoms, and patients' assessment of risk may exist between the two groups and may contribute to differences in outcomes. In addition to clinical differences between groups of women, sociocultural factors require investigation before optimal cardiovascular care can be provided to all groups.

Stroke is the third leading cause of death in the United States and the most important cause of severe disability. The prevalence in women increases with age and for blacks (2). Although men have a higher prevalence of stroke, women have higher mortality (2). Hypertension, diabetes mellitus, cigarette smoking, and cardiac disease are risk factors for stroke, as they are for the development of coronary disease. Although hypertension and diabetes mellitus are not gender-specific risk factors for stroke, they are more prevalent in women than in men. Management of risk factors for stroke and treatment of stroke do not at present appear to differ with gender.

Osteoporosis

Osteoporosis, a loss of bone mass accompanied by increased bone fragility, affects more than 24 million women in the United States. It is estimated that 50% of women older than 45 years and 90% of women older than 75 years have some degree of osteoporosis. Hip fractures occur in some 300,000 American women, and approximately 25% of older women with hip fractures die within 1 year of the fracture (8). Osteoporosis adds $7 billion to $10 billion to the nation's annual medical expenditures. The toll of osteoporosis on the nation's mortality rate and the economy is enormous; moreover, the disease results in prolonged disability and promotes other illnesses. Osteoporosis is of particular importance to women because it is four times as common in women as in men (8). Additionally, hormonal variation during women's life cycles uniquely predisposes them to osteoporosis—menopause or amenorrhea due to nutritional or hormonal causes accelerates bone loss (11). Susceptibility to osteoporosis varies by race, so that black women have lower incidences of osteoporosis than do white and Asian-American women. Because osteoporosis, like cardiovascular disease, is preventable, recognition and modification of risk factors for osteoporosis should be part of the care of women, beginning at adolescence (8,11).

Cancer

Cancer is the second leading cause of death for women, particularly women of color. Five-year survival rates for cancer vary substantially among different ethnic groups of women; 61% of white women survive 5 years after diagnosis of cancer, whereas only 47% of black women survive the same length of time (12). It is important to note that incidence rates of cancer in women do not necessarily parallel mortality rates when they are examined according to ethnic group. For example, black women have incidence rates for breast cancer that are lower than in white women but mortality rates that are higher. Black women also have the highest mortality from cervical cancer, at 7 per 100,000, whereas all other ethnic groups have mortality rates of 3 per 100,000 or fewer (12).

For cancer, as for cardiovascular disease, much research should be directed toward discovering out the relative importance of biological differences among groups of women, as opposed to psychosocial differences, differences in access to care, and differences in physician-patient interactions that might significantly affect women's outcomes.

Human Immunodeficiency Virus Infection

Between 1985 and 1995 in the United States, the proportion of reported AIDS cases in women rose from 7% to 19%; at present AIDS is the third leading cause of death in women ages 25 to 44 years (12). Black women, who make up approximately 12% of the U.S. female population, constitute nearly 68% of all cases of HIV infection and 56% of all cases of AIDS in women. Hispanic women (10% of the general population) account for 6% of all HIV infections and 20% of all cases of AIDS in women. Heterosexual contact and intravenous drug abuse are the two major modes of infection. Women with AIDS are significantly more likely to live in households where others are infected by HIV/AIDS (partners, spouses, or children) and to function in the traditional role of caregiver in circumstances offering little psychosocial support. Such women have shorter survival periods than women who do not experience the stress of being a caregiver under those difficult circumstances. In addition, because women with AIDS often function as family caregivers, the psychosocial devastation to children left parentless when these women die is substantial (12).

Violence Against Women

Violence against women, whether dowry murder, rape as a tool of war, genital mutilation, or domestic violence, is now considered a health care issue as well as a social issue worldwide. In surveys of patients in internal medicine clinics in the United States, 25% to 30% of women had experienced domestic violence as either an adult or a child (13). Despite the risk of serious injury or death, women with a history of violence may often present with multiple health complaints or with psychiatric symptoms instead of being open about their victimization. These victims are more likely to have somatic complaints, as well as a greater prevalence of depression, anxiety, and suicide attempts (13,14). Violence in the home is associated with increased use of the health care system, so primary care physicians should be alert and screen female patients sensitively for a history of domestic violence.

Mood Disorders in Women

In the area of mental health, there are substantial gender differences in disease prevalence. Women have been found to have higher rates of depression and anxiety disorders. This higher prevalence of mood disorders in women appears to hold across racial boundaries (15). A complex amalgam of genetics, life experiences, and societal expectations and stresses, as well as biochemical and neurologic factors across the female life cycle, contributes to the development of mood disorders in women. Treatment of these mental disorders requires research to understand the neurologic, genetic, and biological components, as well as a societal commitment to decrease life stresses that particularly affect women, such as physical and sexual abuse, poverty, racism, and conflict in women's roles as workers and family caregivers.

Women and Clinical Trials

Improvement in the health of all women requires accurate demographic data pinpointing health issues in subgroups of women and clinical research to assess risk factors and treatment responses in these subgroups. Several problems exist in both demographic data collection and the inclusion of women in clinical trials, problems that have resulted in an inadequate knowledge base on which to make management decisions. Failure to include subpopulations in disease surveys can result in underestimation of the true incidence of disease. This was observed when inclusion of blacks in surveys of stroke incidence resulted in an increase in overall stroke prevalence figures. Observational longitudinal studies, such as the Nurses Health Study and the Framingham study, that have ethnically limited populations have led to inadequate understanding of disease incidence and consequences in ethnic groups not represented. Grouping small subpopulations under larger demographic headings (e.g., Hispanic or Asian-Pacific Islander) may actually obscure important health differences. Thus, profound health differences may exist between Mexican Americans and Puerto Ricans (grouped as Hispanic) or between Japanese Americans and people of southeast Asian descent (grouped as Asian-Pacific Islander). Confusion about racial background may also impede the collection of accurate health data (15).

After identification of health problems in demographic surveys, inclusion of diverse groups of women in clinical trials is essential to determining optimal treatment. A critical analysis of why women have been excluded from clinical trials has been summarized by Haseltine in *Women's Health Research* (16). The reasons are as follows:

1. The view that women's health and reproductive health are identical focused early women's health research on maternal/child health. In fact, until 1990, women's health concerns were handled by the National Institute of Child Health and Human Development. Fetal and child health was the primary focus, with maternal health a very secondary concern. Women's health before and after childbearing years was completely ignored.

2. Women's regular hormonal cycles present a confounding variable in clinical trials. To exclude women because of this difficulty, however, is to gloss over the fact that women's diseases must be treated within the context of cyclic hormonal variation, thus data must be collected in such subjects.

3. It has been argued that the cost of clinical research is increased when subgroup analyses must be completed. Avoiding such costs, however, means excluding significant subgroups (e.g., women and minorities), and data thus acquired may not be freely extrapolated to those subgroups. Additional studies become necessary so that the appropriate data can be acquired.

4. The fear of harming pregnant women and their fetuses is a major concern for researchers. Ways to protect fetal health without excluding all women of childbearing age from clinical studies should be sought.

There are additional and very significant barriers to black women's participation in clinical trials. One is the absence of investigators committed to or funded for addressing the health needs of this segment of the population. The absence of accurate disease prevalence data prevents the placement of proper health emphasis within minority communities. Inadequate health care facilities within black communities, where clinical research is not likely to be based, make recruitment and management of clinical research subjects difficult. Black women are less likely to trust scientists to behave ethically or to think that investigators would care for them appropriately (17). To reduce these barriers, it is essential that minority investigators function as leaders of clinical trials, that clinical trials be based within minority communities, and that stringent safeguards be observed to protect women and minority clinical research subjects. Until sufficient numbers of women of diverse backgrounds are included in clinical trials, data guiding treatments in these subgroups will be lacking, and minority women in particular will be denied optimal health care.

REFERENCES

1. *Women's health in the curriculum: a resource guide for faculty.* National Academy on Women's Health Medical Education, 1996.
2. Mosca L, Manson J, Sutherland S, Langer R, Manolio T, Barrett-Connor E. Cardiovascular disease in women: a statement for healthcare professionals from the American Heart Association. *Circulation* 1997;96:2468–2482.
3. Jacobs S, Sherwood J. Heart and mind: the practice of cardiac psychology: the cardiac psychology of women and coronary heart disease. *CVR&R* 1997;August:32–52.

 4. Stampfer MJ, Colditz G. Estrogen replacement therapy and coronary heart disease: a quantitative assessment of the epidemiologic evidence. *Prev Med* 1991;20:47–63.
 5. Grodstein F, Stampfer M, Manson J, et al. Postmenopausal estrogen and progestin use and the risk of cardiovascular disease. *N Engl J Med* 1996;335:453–461.
 6. Gerhard M, Ganz P. How do we explain the clinical benefit of estrogen? From bedside to bench. *Circulation* 1995;92:5–8.
 7. Vogel R, Corretti M. Estrogens, progestins and heart disease. Can endothelial function divine the benefit? *Circulation* 1998;97:1223–1226.
 8. Healy B. *Getting the best medical care in a man's world: a new prescription for women's health.* New York: Penguin, 1995.
 9. Lerner DJ, Kannel WB. Patterns of coronary disease morbidity and mortality in the sexes: a 26 year follow-up of the Framingham population. *Am Heart J* 1986;111:383.
10. Tofler GH, Stone PH, Muller JE, et al. Effects of gender and race on prognosis after myocardial infarction: adverse prognosis for women, particularly black women. *J Am Coll Cardiol* 1987;9:473–482.
11. Eastell R. Treatment of postmenopausal osteoporosis. *N Engl J Med* 1998;338:736–746.
12. Leigh WA. *Women of color health data book: adolescents to seniors.* Bethesda, MD: Office of Research on Women's Health, Office of the Director, National Institutes of Health; 1998; NIH publication no. 98-4247.
13. McCauley J, Kern D, Kolodner K, et al. The "battering syndrome": prevalence and clinical characteristics of domestic violence in primary care internal medicine practices. *Ann Intern Med* 1995;123:737–746.
14. Caralis P, Musialowski R. Women veterans' and nonveterans' experiences with domestic violence. *Fed Practitioner* 1997;December:21–34.
15. Russo N. *Women's mental health: research agenda for the twenty-first century.* Pittsburgh: University of Pittsburgh Press, 1995:373–396.
16. Haseltine F, ed. *Women's health research: a medical and policy primer.* Society for the Advancement of Women's Health Research, 1997:13–17.
17. Mouton C, Harris S, Ravi S, Solorzano P, Johnson M. Barriers to black women's participation in cancer clinical trials. *J Natl Med Assoc* 1997;89:721–727.

Subject Index

Note: Page numbers followed by *f* indicate figures; page numbers followed by *t* indicate tables.

A

Abbott, Major, 8, 9f
Acquired immunodeficiency syndrome, in
        women, 89
Adenoviruses, 20
Angiogenesis, 24–25
Anti-Kickback Act, 58–59
Anticipatory guidance, 59–60
Arrhythmias, caused by cocaine use, 41
Augusta, A. T., 8–9

B

Biopsychosocial influences on health, 29–38
    socioeconomic status, 30–35. *See also*
        Socioeconomic status, effect
        of on health
Black medical schools, 9–11
Black physicians, contributions of, 8–11
    Abbott, Major, 8, 9f
    Augusta, A. T., 8–9
    Boylston, Zabdiel, 8
    Cesar, 8
    Degrasse, John V., 8, 9f
    Delaney, Martin Robison, 8, 9f
    Derham, James, 8
    Drew, Charles R., 9, 10f
    Howard, Edward C., 8, 9f
    Imhotep, 8
    Johnson, John Beauregard, 9, 11f
    Onesimus, 8
    Papan, 8
    Peck, David John, 8
    Primus, 8
    Ray, Peter W., 8, 9f
    Santomee, Lucas, 8
    Smith, James McCune, 8, 9f
    Williams, Daniel Hale, 9, 10f
Black-related diseases, 11–14
    congenital, 12
    environmental, 12–13
    genetic, 12
    idiopathic, 13–14

    infectious, 13
    oncogenic, 13
Blacks
    disease resistance in, 14
    female
        cardiovascular disease in, 88
        and clinical trials, 91
        response to hypertension medications by, 14,
            15f, 78–82
Boylston, Zabdiel, 8

C

Cancer
    incidence of in blacks, 13
    in women, 89
Cardiac hypertrophy, and molecular genetics
    acquired, 22–23
    hereditary, 21–22
Cardiomyopathy, caused by cocaine use, 41
Cardiovascular disease. *See also* Molecular
        genetics and cardiovascular disease
    in women, 86–88
      in blacks, 88
      and poor outcome after myocardial infarc-
        tion, 87, 88
      and postmenopausal hormone replacement
        therapy, 87
      risk factors for, 87
      stroke, 88
Cesar, 8
Cocaine abuse, 39–43
    arrhythmias caused by, 41
    cardiomyopathy caused by, 41
    cerebrovascular accident caused by,
        40–41
    management of, 42
    myocardial infarction caused by, 40
    pharmacology and pharmacokinetics of,
        39–40
    in pregnancy, 41–42, 41t
Consent, 60
Culture, effect of in medicine, 6, 7, 7f

D

Degrasse, John V., 8, 9f
Delaney, Martin Robison, 8, 9f
Derham, James, 8
Dietary Approaches to Stop Hypertension, 70
DNA, structure and function of, 18
Drew, Charles R., 9, 10f
Duty of continuing care, 59–60

E

Education, medical. *See* Ethics, medical, and
    medical education
Enhancers, in gene expression, 19
Estrogen replacement therapy, and cardiovascu-
    lar disease in women, 87
Ethics, medical, and medical education, 47–52
    in continuing education, 51
    Eurocentrism of, 49
    at Howard University, 50
    introduction of courses on, 48
Ethnicity
    effect of in medicine, 5–6, 7, 7f
    and socioeconomic status and health,
        31–32, 33f
        and environmental exposures, 32, 34
        and physiologic processes, 34–35
        and psychological and behavioral factors, 34

F

False Claims Act, 55–59
    billing as target of, 57
    employer-employee relationship as target of,
        57–58
    and lack of requirement of proof of criminal
        intent, 56
    referrals as target of (Anti-Kickback Act), 58–59
    Stark Bill, 59
Fibroblast growth factors, 24–25
Flexner Report on Medical Education, 11
Fraud in health care, 53–55

G

Genes. *See also* Molecular genetics and cardio-
    vascular disease
    defects in, 19–20
    expression of, 18–19
    manipulations of, 20–21
    structure of, 18

H

Health care reform, and persistence of link
        between socioeconomic status
        and health, 31

Hormone replacement therapy, and cardiovascu-
    lar disease in women, 87
Howard, Edward C., 8, 9f
Howard University, medical ethics course at, 50
Human immunodeficiency virus, in women, 89
Hypercholesterolemia, familial, gene-based
        therapy for, 23–24
Hypertension
    in blacks, 12–13, 73–82
    drug therapy for
        effectiveness of vs. that in whites, 14,
            15f, 78–82
        studies by Materson et al. on,
            78–79, 79f
        study by Hall and Kong on, 80, 80f
        selection of based on race, 77
    increased incidence of, 73–74
    pathophysiology of vs. that of whites,
        74–77, 77t
        cardiac and hemodynamic para-
            meters, 75
        cellular parameters, 76
        dietary factors, 76
        endocrine and metabolic factors, 75–76
        genetics, 76–77
        neurogenic factors, 74–75
        obesity, 76
        psychosocial stressors, 74
        renal mechanisms, 75
        vascular mechanisms, 75
    Dietary Approaches to Stop Hypertension, 70

I

Imhotep, 8
Insurance companies, and fight against fraud, 60

J

Johnson, John Beauregard, 9, 11f

L

Lead poisoning, increased incidence of in
        blacks, 13
Legal issues in medicine, 53–62
    consent, 60
    enforcement, 60
    False Claims Act, 55–59. *See also* False
        Claims Act
    Medicare fraud, 53–55
    negligence, 59–60. *See also* Negligence
    protective measures for physicians, 61–62
    rights of physicians when investigated, 60–61
Linnaeus, racial classification by, 2, 3
Lipid reduction, gene-based therapy for, 23–24

M

Malpractice. *See* Legal issues in medicine
Medical ethics. *See* Ethics, medical, and med-
    ical education
Medicare fraud, 53–55
Molecular genetics and cardiovascular disease,
        17–27. *See also* Genes
    animal models, 20–21
    in cardiac hypertrophy
        acquired, 22–23
        hereditary, 21–22
    in congenital heart disease, 23
    gene-based therapies, 23–25
        for angiogenesis, 24–25
        for lipid reduction, 23–24
        for myocardial infarction as a myocyte-
            deficiency disease, 25
        for restenosis, 24
Morton, Samuel George, linking of intelligence
        and skull size by, 2–4
Mutations, genetic, 19–20
Myocardial infarction
    caused by cocaine use, 40
    gene-based therapy for, 25
    and poor outcome in women, 87, 88
Myocarditis, caused by cocaine use, 41

N

Negligence, 59–60
    and duty of continuing care (anticipatory
        guidance), 59–60
    and establishment of doctor-patient relation-
        ship, 59
Nutrition in minorities, 63–72
    and curative medical perspective, 66–67
    and deaths from diet-related chronic diseases,
        63–66, 64t, 65f
    and hypertension, 76
    lack of courses on in medical education, 66
    lack of physician attention to, 66
    public health paradigm and, 67–70
        "biochemical individuality," 69
        consumer perceptions of diet and
            health, 70
        culture and psychosocial factors in food
            choice, 69–70
        diabetes and "thrifty genotype" hypothe-
            sis, 68–69
    risk reduction through dietary intervention,
        70–71
        CARDES, 71
        Dietary Approaches to Stop Hyper-
            tension, 70

O

Office of Behavioral and Social Sciences
        Research of NIH, 29–30
Onesimus, 8
Osteoporosis, 88–89

P

Papan, 8
Peck, David John, 8
Polymorphism, 19–20
Poverty and health. *See* Socioeconomic status,
        effect of on health
Primus, 8
Promoters, in gene expression, 19

R

Race. *See also* Black-related diseases; Blacks;
        Hypertension
    classifications of, 1–4, 2t, 3f
        by skin color, 2
        by skull size, 2–4, 4t
    effect of in medicine, 1–5, 7, 7f
Ray, Peter W., 8, 9f
Religion, effect of in medicine, 6–7, 7f
Restenosis, gene-based therapy for, 24
Retroviruses, 20
Rheumatic fever, increased incidence of in
        blacks, 13
RNA, structure and function of, 18

S

Santomee, Lucas, 8
Sarcoidosis, increased incidence of in blacks,
        13–14
Sickle cell anemia, 12
Skin color, classification of humans by, 2
Slavery, "scientific" justifications of, 3–4
Smith, James McCune, 8, 9f
Smoking cessation, behavioral techniques for, 36
Socioeconomic status, effect of on health, 30–35
    and access to health care, 31
    behavioral interventions for, 35–36
        smoking cessation, 36
        stress management techniques, 35
    and ethnicity, 31–32, 33f
        and environmental exposures, 32, 34
        and physiologic processes, 34–35
        and psychological and behavioral
            factors, 34
    factors linking, 30–31, 32t
Stark Bill, 59
Stress management techniques, 35
Stroke, in women, 88